Complimetry Copy.

To: Higgins
     with best wishes
         Joseph R. Spies
           Arlington, VA
              Nov. 2, 1993

BIG CATS

and other animals.

Their Beauty, Dignity and Survival

by

Dr. Joseph R. Spies

White Tiger

For information address:
Frederick Fell Publishers, Inc.
2131 Hollywood Blvd.
Hollywood, Florida 33020

International Standard Book No. 0-8119-0737-6
Library of Congress Catalog Card No. 88-045464

Published simultaneously in Canada by
Book Center Inc., Montreal, Quebec, H4R 1R8

2 3 4 5 6 7 8 9 0

This book is dedicated to:

The memory of Thornton W. Burgess, whose stories nurtured my early love of animals; preservation of animals and their natural habitats; and fostering the practice of the Golden Rule in our relationships with our animal friends.

ACKNOWLEDGMENTS

I thank the following animal keepers and administrative persons for their kind consideration during my ten-year period of zoo animal photography: Kehinde Adeduji, Ilene Berg, Melanie Bond, Lisa Burton, Kayce Cover, Frank Cusimano, Bess Frank, Susanne Frank, Curley Harper, Jim Jones, Jim Lillie, Mike Morgan, Vincent Rico, Miles Roberts, Bill Rose, Cynthia Sommerfeld and Lisa Stevens. All of the animal keepers had genuine love and respect for the animals in their care. My thanks too to the many workers and volunteers in FONZ (Friends of the National Zoo) and the National Zoological Park of the Smithsonian Institution for their dedicated service to animals. It is to these that we are indebted for maintenance of this beautiful zoo.

PREFACE

Humans have the power of life and death over all other creatures of the earth, including man himself. With this power, goes responsibility for the welfare of animals. Animals deserve our respect because they have survived longer than man has without all of the advantages.

Zoos play a very important role in educating the public in appreciation of animals leading to creation and/or maintenance of natural ecosystems where animals can coexist with man without constant danger of extinction.

I have been a frequent visitor to the National Zoological Park in Washington, D.C., since my retirement as a research scientist several years ago. Animal photography has been my avocation for many years. I came to feel that through photography, I could make a small, though positive, contribution to educating the public to appreciate animals. Consequently, the purpose of this book is to educate by illustrating the beauty and dignity of animals by capturing them in photographs. These photographs also illustrate the advances made toward providing a more natural environment for zoo animals and the dividend accrued in healthier and happier animals compared with that in their old, cramped, uncomfortable quarters. This can be shown in the photographs where natural backgrounds can be obtained with a little effort on the photographer's part.

It took millions of years to evolve the wonderful variety of animals of the world. Let us learn to appreciate and not destroy them in a few careless years. Let us change our attitudes and actions so we can live in harmony with our animal friends, and pass on this marvelous heritage to future generations.

This work is not presented as definitive with respect to coverage of animals. Rather, it depends on the qualities of a few animals captured in photographs to illustrate that array of characteristics that makes animals so appealing for their own sakes and not as sources of economic gain. The photographs in this book were taken at the National Zoological Park, Washington, D.C., except for a few as noted.

Table Of Contents

INTRODUCTION

Extinction lasts forever. It is sad to contemplate the extinction of an animal species due to the inexorable forces of nature. But, it is infinitely more depressing when the extinction is caused by supposedly responsible human beings.

The treatment of animals by some people is appalling. For example, a person who wears the fur of an endangered animal or uses other products derived from elephants, rhinoceroses, gorillas and the like is guilty of insensitivity, ignorance and weak submission to peer pressure for the sake of vanity. The act of wearing furs by otherwise civilized people is all so unnecessary because natural (wool) and synthetic products are available for warmth. Synthetic furs rival natural furs in beauty.

The fine lady or handsome gentleman who proudly wears a fur coat can be forgiven because of their ignorance. But those who kill for sport are near the bottom on the scale of human values. The spectacle of one of these attempting to demonstrate his macho prowess by exhibiting a photograph with his foot atop a dead lion or elephant, which he killed from a safe distance with a high-powered rifle, is utterly contemptible. No less contemptible are those who kill or maim lesser creatures merely for the thrill of it. George Bernard Shaw, during the 1960s, openly expressed his disgust after viewing a newspaper photograph of a famous macho author, rifle in hand, with foot atop a dead lion. Paraphrased, his pithy comment was that an artist who paints a beautiful bird or stalks a live animal in his native liberty with a camera, is a thousand times better sportsman than the malignant idiot who shoots them and then gets photographed sitting on the corpse. Shaw was too mild in his comment. He should have said 'is an infinitely better sportsman than ___ .'

On a more optimistic note, there is some hope that the trend toward animal extinction can be stopped or even reversed. There is an increasing number of groups dedicated to stemming the tide of animal destruction. Among these groups are the international zookeepers. Both the objectives and facilities of zoos have changed dramatically during the past few decades. Originally, zoos consisted of closely confined animals kept solely for the entertainment of spectators. Minimum consideration was given to the comfort and well-being of the animals. Gradually, this limited objective was broadened. Now, living quarters for the animals are designed to increase their comfort by placing them in a more natural setting. The animals have responded by being happier and more relaxed in their new surroundings. Education and greater appreciation of animals, not entertainment, are now the emphasis.

Another increasingly important function of zoos is to provide a last refuge for animals facing extinction in the wild. The breeding and refuge programs of zoos are regarded by many as more important than the educational programs. Regardless of their respective merits, both programs are vital to attempts to save the animals of the world. At present, it is doubtful that financial support will be sufficient to maintain the breeding program alone.

Zoos, per se, cannot provide long-term preservation of endangered species. They do not have the facilities nor the financial resources to support populations of sufficient size to overcome the results of inbreeding. Inbreeding causes loss of the genetic diversity required to maintain the animals. It also results in loss of fertility, production of still-born or deformed offspring and general physical deterioration of surviving offspring. Carnivores and the larger herbivores are more susceptible to deterioration due to inbreeding than some ungulates and birds.

Notwithstanding these limitations, the role of zoos in conservation can be substantial. Zoos can provide a temporary haven for endangered species. Here, they can be studied with the ultimate objective of introducing them back into their natural habitats. Zoos can also play a very important role in educating the public to appreciate rare animals and create and maintain natural ecosystems where endangered species can truly be preserved.

Bengal Tiger

CHAPTER I

Origin And History Of Cats And Other Mammals

If I had to choose, I would select cats as my favorite animal. Consequently, although this historical account emphasizes the evolution of the felines, it is also generally applicable to all mammals.

There are approximately 5,000 known living species of mammals (vertebrates which suckle their young) that are divided into 18 orders. The families comprising the Carnivora, or flesh eater, order include: the cats, the dogs, the hyenas, the bears, the raccoons, the coatis and pandas, the martens, the badgers, the skunks, the otters, the civets and mongooses, the seals, the sea lions and the walruses.

The cat family (Felidae) is among the best of the carnivores in evolutionary adaptation to their environment. For example, the cheetah is capable of speeds up to 70 miles an hour in capturing its prey. The lion is slower, but stronger and more cunning in hunting its prey. The top speed of the domestic cat is 30 miles an hour. All cats are well-equipped with fangs and claws for killing and eating flesh. The cats and dogs are the best known of the carnivora. The cat, **Felis catus**, is among the smallest members of the cat family which contains lions, tigers, leopards and jaguars as its largest members.

Whence came the cat? The earth is estimated to be 4½ billion years old. Life began on earth about 2 billion years ago. The history of the early inhabitants of the earth is obtained from studying the fossils. The earliest animal fossils are those of primitive water invertebrates which inhabited the ancient seas. Fossil records show that the first fishes appeared about 425 million years ago and the first amphibians 365 million years ago. The oldest fossil egg is 280 million years old. Propagation of these early life forms was undoubtedly inefficient and dependent on the survival of a few of the huge numbers produced. Then, between 280 and 100 million years ago creatures evolved which suckled their young. Finally, the placenta evolved. The placenta consists of a membrane and system of blood vessels by which the embryo can be nourished while developing inside the mother's body. These evolutionary developments provided the advantage needed to ensure the survival, diversification and increase of mammals. However, it took 27 million years more, during which the dominant reptiles began to disappear, before the mammals fully came into their own, even with their superior propagation equipment.

The Paleocene epoch, which lasted from about 63 to 58 million years ago, witnessed the final extinction of the ruling reptiles and the beginning of the age of mammals.

During the Eocene epoch (58 to 36 million years ago), various carnivores developed. Cat-like animals are thought to have originated from the **Miacia**, an elongated, weasel-like creature. During this epoch, the primates, the forerunners of man, also developed. The ancestors of man and the domestic cat had their origins in the same geologic age and commenced their savage and relentless struggle for survival.

The mammals continued to flourish during the Oligocene epoch, 36 to 25 million years ago. Efficient life forms evolved further and those with weaker mental and physical equipment became extinct. The big cats of this epoch, such as **Dinictis**, were surprisingly similar to modern cats. Dinictis was about the size of a lynx, with cat-like teeth, retractile claws, but a very small brain. These early cats, including Dinictis, had canine teeth that were much larger than those of modern cats. From this origin, cats took two different pathways in the evolution of their teeth. In one, the upper canines grew larger, culminating in the saber-toothed tigers. In the other, the canine teeth became smaller as in modern cats. The saber-toothed tigers were heavy, slow-moving with large foreparts and relatively small hindquarters. The largest and best-known saber-toothed tiger was **Smilodon** which was about the size of a lion with canine teeth six inches in length. Smilodon became extinct only a few thousand years ago. The bones of hundreds of these tigers have been found in the LaBrea tar pits in Los Angeles, Calif.

The Oligocene merged into the Miocene epoch which is known as the "golden age" of mammals. Many species of cats of various sizes inhabited the earth during this period, millions of years before the appearance of man. About 50 of these species are now extinct, and about 37 species (the domestic cat is a single species) are currently in existence in all parts of the world. In the late miocene epoch, however, the mammals started to decline with the exception of the primates which continued to evolve into higher, and more successful forms.

At the outset of the "age of mammals," many primates, including tree shrews, tarsiers, and lemurs, were already well-established tree dwellers. Successful tree-dwelling required superior physical and mental adaptations to those required for walking on the ground. Consequently, when these primates returned to the ground in the miocene epoch, these adaptations gave them an important advantage over the ground-dwelling animals. Their well-developed brains and powers of coordination led to superior intelligence. It was intelligence, imagination and development of emotions that set these ancestors of man apart from the other mammals, and accounted for man's comparatively rapid evolution in terms of the geologic time scale.

Man made his appearance in the last million or few million years, during what is known as the Pleistocene epoch. The Pleistocene epoch has been characterized by violent climatic changes. Four times, arctic weather was imposed on much of the earth by the ice sheets that descended from the polar regions driving most of the living creatures before it. The last ice sheet began its retreat only 10,000 years ago.

The severe conditions imposed by the ice ages and competition from man accelerated the further decline of the mammals. Survival in these changing environments, according to the laws of biological survival, required that the species either move to a new place with a climate similar to that where they developed or adapt to the new climate. The magnificently equipped saber-tooths evidently were unable to adjust and thus became extinct a few thousand years ago. However, concurrently, other members of the cat family and the primate groups did survive. Their paths converged one step nearer to their destined historical meeting and modern relationship with man.

What prompted the first associations of cat (ancestors of the domestic cat) and man in the vastness of these pre-historic times? Was it a slight mutual advantage that helped tip the balance in their favor in the long struggles for survival? Or, was the first attraction of an aesthetic nature? When did the first associations occur? We can only speculate on these questions because firm answers cannot be given. Perhaps associations of cat and man occurred for different reasons at different times. Undoubtedly, over the years, man and cat found themselves, involuntarily, up the same tree attempting to escape a common enemy. Certainly this association had a mutual-survival motive. Perhaps, man and cat found themselves in the same cave to escape storms and biting cold. Perhaps a child brought home a tiny, helpless, motherless kitten and the first glimmer of human kindness led the family to feed and care for the little animal. The child's natural affection would do the rest to induce the family to keep the kitten as a pet. Perhaps aesthetic appreciation of the cat as a pet gradually developed through repeated experiences of this kind. Then too, early man learned to appreciate the practical value of the cat in preventing rodent damage to supplies.

The author feels that the affection inherent in children and women was the most important element in the "domestication" of the cat. This view is supported by a study of the customs of today's primitive peoples and the behavior of wild animals. For example, women and children of hunting tribes such as the Guayaki of South America and various aborigines of Australia, enjoy making pets of small animals and birds, even though these pets are a burden because of the limited food supplies of these tribes, always on the move in search of game. It seems likely that man has long had a deep affection for animals. In fact, closer study of their pet animals might have been helpful to the tribe in learning of wild members of the species, and thus helpful in hunting them for food.

Yet another factor in cat/man associations may have been the attraction of scraps of food left by man at his campsite or an occasional morsel tossed to a hungry cat in the vicinity of the camp.

The domestic cat will mate with Asiatic, African and European wildcats. This is an indication that these species were among its forebearers. In contrast, the North American wildcat does not mate with the domestic cat. In fact, it is an enemy of the domestic cat, killing it when possible. No small cat similar to the domestic cat originated in North America.

White Tiger and Bengal Tiger Cub

CHAPTER II

The Cat Family

The familiar domestic cat is a smaller member of the cat family, which includes the lesser known big cats, such as the tiger, the lion, the leopard, and the intermediate-sized wild cats. The cat family will be discussed comparatively with the domestic cat.

Living things are classified on the basis of convenience and of natural relationships, especially common descent. The latter basis stems primarily from the publication of Charles Darwin's "Origin of the Species," (1859). The zoological classification of the cat family, and particularly the domestic cat, is shown in Table 2.1.

Table 2.1
Taxonomy of the Domestic Cat

Phylum:	Chordata
Class:	Mammal
Order:	Carnivora
Family:	Felidae
Genus:	Felis
Species:	Catus
Scientific Name:	Felis catus, Linnaeus
Common Name:	Domestic cat

The classification of members of the cat family (Felids) by zoologists has been controversial. In general, much of the classification of mammals is based on the relative proportions of different parts of the skull. These proportions are remarkably similar in Felids, despite great variations in their size. However, variations in the color markings of Felids, ranging from a single color to a complex combination of stripes, spots and blotches, has lead to the controversy. The number of genera proposed for Felidae has ranged from two to 23. Ernest P. Walker in the book, "Mammals of the World," (1964) has classified Felidae into six genera consisting of about 37 species.

The distribution of Felids is almost worldwide, except for Australia, Antarctica, West Indies and some oceanic islands. Although no Felids are indigenous to Australia, there are five species of marsupials, called *native cats,* in Australia, New Guinea and Tasmania. These *native cats* bear a slight resemblance to true cats.

Felids have a variety of forms, but from the largest lions and tigers down to the smallest jungle cats, including domestic cats, all are remarkably similar in basic structure and characteristics. The largest Felid is the tiger, which reaches a weight of up to 600 pounds, a height of five feet and an overall length of 14 feet. The next largest, the lion, seldom exceeds 400 pounds, a height of 4½ feet and a length of 9 feet. Male pumas average 160 to 175 pounds, although pumas up to 200 pounds have been reported. The combined length of the head and body of members of the cat family ranges from 19½ to 146 inches and the weight ranges from 5½ to 600 pounds. Felids are powerfully built, muscular, supple and compact and characterized by rounded heads and short muzzles. They have large, highly-developed brains and excellent coordination.

The length of the tail ranges from none for the Manx up to three feet for members of the genus Panthera. It has been suggested that the function of the tail is to aid in balancing, and that skillful use of the tail accounts for the ability of many Felids to land on their feet when falling. This function of the tail has been questioned, and it was suggested that this ability may be due to the structure of their semi-circular ear canals. Lending credence to this theory is the fact that the tailless Manx can make the turn while falling as successfully as cats with tails. Possibly, the great muscular coordination and quick reflexes of the cat contribute to its ability to always land on its feet.

The primary function of the tail on felids is for displaying emotions and as an intimidation weapon. Tail erections, wavings, thumpings, and swishings are used by males as a threat in rivalry against other males of the species. Also an erect, bushy tail, accompanied by an arched back and bristling hair increases the apparent size and serves as a bluff in an attempt to frighten an enemy or rival into thinking it is dealing with a larger and fiercer animal. The author has observed that pet cats, content and at ease, use the tail to acknowledge conversation or caresses. This display involves a very gentle flip of the tip of the tail.

The legs of the Felids are usually stocky but can range to slender and sinewy, as demonstrated in the cheetah. The forefoot has five digits and the hind foot four. Domestic cats with more than 18 toes are not uncommon. Cats are digitigrade; that is, they walk or trot on their toes.

The feet of Felids are covered with hair, except the pads, in order to silently stalk prey. The claws are strong, sharp, and recurved to hold living prey. The claws are retractile; that is, they are sheathed when not being used to prevent breaking and blunting by excessive contact with rocks and the ground. When the claws are unsheathed, at will, the toes are spread apart making the foot about twice as broad as normal, thus converting the foot into either a lethal fighting weapon or efficient tool for climbing and holding food. All Felids have this claw sheath, except for the cheetah whose claws are only semi-retractile. Claws grow like fingernails, and Felids like to keep their front claws trimmed. Back claws are trimmed by biting. They exercise their paws by pulling against tree trunks or other strong material.

Another highly specialized characteristic of Felids is their sharp teeth which are used for stabbing and cutting. Stabbing is done with the canine teeth which are elongate, sharply pointed, and slightly recurved. These teeth extend well beyond the other teeth. The canines make deep puncture wounds and are used for killing prey. Cutting is done toward the back of the mouth with the fourth premolars in the upper jaw and the first molars of the lower jaw. The cutting teeth are called carnassials. They are used for cutting prey into pieces small enough to swallow. The rest of the teeth are not very functional as most of them do not even meet. Another characteristic of Felids is that they have no crushing teeth and, therefore can only cut up food, instead of chewing it.

Bengal Tiger

Cheetah

The surface of the tongue of Felids is covered with sharp, recurved, horny papillae which are used for retaining food within the mouth (especially liquids), licking flesh from the bone and grooming the coat. It is said that the large cats can draw blood just with their rasp-like tongues.

The eyes of Felids are of two types. In the genus Panthera, and some of the genus Felis, the pupils remain round on contraction. But in most of the members of Felis, including the domestic cat, the pupils contract to narrow vertical slits, becoming round as they open. The size of the opening varies with the intensity of the light. Cats cannot see in total darkness, but they are sensitive to very faint light owing to the ability of the pupil to form a large aperture.

Whiskers of Felids are long and well-developed. They have a sensory function in guiding movement in darkness. Some species of cats are nocturnal and some diurnal. The domestic cat is both nocturnal and diurnal.

Purring is one of the best known characteristics of the domestic cat. Other members of the genus Felis also possess this characteristic. Purring is a distinctive, continuous, rising and falling murmur associated with pleasure and contentment. Purring is not related to the voice of the animal. The vibration frequency of purring is much lower than that of the vocal cords. The fact that some species of Felids, in which the hyoid bones are incomplete, are unable to purr indicates that the whole hyoid-laryngeal structure vibrates to produce the purr. The hyoid bone forms the support for the tongue and gives origin to muscles passing to the tongue and larynx. It also supports the thyroid cartilage. Felidae may be divided into two groups on the basis of the hyoid bone structure. In one group of cats, the epihyal (normally one of four cartilage-

Leopard

Atlas Lion

linked bones of the hyoid composing the cranial cornu) fails to develop beyond a thread-like ligament so that the tongue and larynx are only loosely
attached to the base of the skull. This group constitutes the genus Panthera
(tiger, lion, leopard and jaguar) which are unable to purr. Their voices are a
roar. In the second group (genus felis) the epihyal develops to normal bony
structure and all these cats can purr but not roar. The cheetah has a normal
hyoid structure and can, therefore, purr.

Felids are usually solitary animals. But sometimes they travel in pairs, as
family groups or with the lion, in "prides" of sometimes as many as 20 or 30
members. They stalk their prey or lie in wait and then attempt to seize the
victim in a great burst of speed. Felids bound in great leaps when running at
full speed, especially when running in high grass. The lion's leap measures 21
feet.

The large Felids range over large areas. The mountain lion, or puma, is
reported to range over an area 13 miles in diameter.

Felids have an acute sense of smell, sight and hearing. Their prey consists
of other mammals as well as birds, reptiles and even fish. Panthera may prey
on livestock and even human beings. Tigers that are old, wounded or otherwise incapable of killing their usual prey, sometimes turn to killing man and
have to be destroyed. Professional hunters are usually called on to do this.

The Panthera have tremendous strength. The leopard frequently stores its
uneaten prey in a tree. A piece of a young buffalo that weighed about 100
pounds was cached in an acacia tree about 11 feet above the ground by a
leopard. The great strength of the mature tiger is well known. It has been
reported that a tiger moved a buffalo about 49 feet. Thirteen men were unable
to drag this carcass.

10

Jaguar

Felids are excellent swimmers when the need arises. Tigers especially are fond of water. The fishing cat lives on lakesides and riversides. The Abyssinian breed of domestic cat is especially fond of water.

Felids typically take refuge in trees, caves, burrows, or natural vegetation. They defend themselves with tooth and claw or they run and hide from danger. Normally, their facial expression is serene and pleasant. But, when they are angry, they have a frightening appearance as they hiss and make blood-curdling cries. They also attempt to frighten an enemy by arching their back and bristling their hair so that they seem twice their normal size. Felids are among the quickest-reacting and fastest-moving of the mammals. They can transform instantly from a state of peaceful relaxation to fighting fury or high-speed action. The cheetah is best known for its speed of up to 70 miles an hour when charging its prey.

There are two other African cats which have tremendous speed but are less well-known than the cheetah. The caracal is smaller than the cheetah but has almost as much speed in running. Caracals are reported to be so fast in their movements that when let loose in a flock of pigeons on the ground they have been known to kill half dozen or more and then spring six feet into the air to capture another one. The serval is another cat of slender build like the cheetah, but it too is smaller. It has great ground speed and travels through high grass in long, high bounds. The serval, like the caracal, often catches birds that it has flushed into the air or that are perched up to nine feet above ground. The

Serval

serval is a fast and agile climber that can catch hyraxes (essentially arboreal animals) in trees. The serval is a fierce fighter and is able to kill dogs. Instant reflex action, high ground speed, and skillful climbing ability, undoubtedly are evolutionary developments that have contributed much to the survival of Felids for so many years.

Puberty in most Felids is reached at an age of 12 to 15 months (slightly less in the domestic cat). Gestation ranges from 55 to 113 days, although it has been reported to be nine months in the jaguarundi. Gestation averages 63 days in the domestic cat. Females of most members of the genus Felis come into heat several times a year. Most Felids have one or two litters per year, although the larger ones sometimes have only one litter every two or three years. The size of litters in most members of Felis genus is from one to six; usually two to four. At birth, Felids are usually blind and helpless, but they do have hair. Felids live up to 30 years, although the life span of the domestic cat is usually little more than half of this.

The intricate combination of bone and muscle in the cat's body accounts for its remarkable physical efficiency. This physical marvel is the product of millions of years of evolutionary development. The skeleton and musculature of the domestic cat is representative of all Felids. There are more than 500 voluntary muscles in the domestic cat. The skeleton of this cat has 230 to 247 bones. These bones are distributed as follows: head, 35-40; vertebral column, 52-53, including 21 to 23 tail bones; ribs, 26; sternum, 1-8; pelvis 2-8, upper extremeties, 62; lower extremeties, 54-56. The number of bones varies with age, older cats have fewer than younger ones because in the older animal, some bones that were originally separate have grown together. There are two main reasons for the cat's supple body movements—the shoulder joint is relatively open, allowing the cat to turn its foreleg in almost any direction; and, the cat's clavicle is either very small or absent, thus permitting greater freedom of movement of the foreleg.

The digestive system of the cat, like that of man, consists of mouth, esophagus, stomach, duodenum, small and large intestines and rectum. However, unlike man, the salivary juices of the cat are deficient in ptyalin, the enzyme that hydrolyzes starches into their component monosaccharidic sugars. Therefore, starches are not digested until they reach the small intestines where digestion is probably negligible. The protein-digesting enzymes of the cat's stomach are very potent, they can soften bone in about an hour.

The cat's normal body temperature is 101.5°F (38.6°C); the heart beats 120 (110 to 140) times per minute in the adult and 168 to 300 times per minute in newborn kittens; the breathing rate is 26 times per minute.

The cat has 30 permanent teeth, 16 in the upper jaw and 14 in the lower jaw. The number of primary or milk teeth is 24. The milk teeth are replaced by the permanent teeth at about five months of age.

The voices of Felids are very expressive. In the domestic cat alone, 30 to 100 different kinds of vocal expressions have been recognized by those studying the cat's voice. Aside from the familiar meow, of which there are many variations, there are trills, distinctive mating calls, hisses, spittings, snarls, growls, and screams. Abilities of various species of cats to purr or roar was discussed earlier in the book.

The tail of the cat may be long, short, bobbed, kinked, curled, or absent.

There are long-haired, short-haired, and rex or curly-haired cats. The coat thickens in winter and sheds or thins in summer. The coat is groomed by the cat by licking or washing with the tongue.

The female domestic cat first comes into heat between six and ten months of age. The female is polyestrous; that is, she comes into heat intermittently and irregularly, and the period lasts anywhere from three days to three weeks. Most females "call" when in heat; that is, they have a peculiar series of cries to attract the male. They also indulge in rolling and other antics to attract the male. Prime breeding age is from two to eight years, but good kittens have been produced by much older females. It is reported that a cat has been bred at 25 years of age.

The gestation period ranges from 52 to 69 days, with the average being 62-63 days. Litters range from one to six, with two to four most frequent.

Kittens are born blind and helpless, although sometimes Siamese are born with their eyes open. The time required for kittens to open their eyes varies, but it is usually about seven to ten days. Kittens nurse from six to eight weeks and mature in five to eight months.

The average life expectancy of the cat has historically been about 12 to 14 years, but with advances in feeding, care and veterinary medicine, the life expectancy is now 17 years. Authenticated cases of cats living beyond 30 years have been reported, with 34 years probably the record. The author had a cat that lived 18 years.

The foregoing information on the ubiquitous domestic cat provides insight into the physical makeup, temperament and behavior of many other members—large and small—of the cat family.

CHAPTER III

Camouflage

Disguise, or camouflage, by protective coloration and design has been an essential factor in survival of both predators and prey. The evolutionary development of protective disguises is strikingly evident in the cat family. Undoubtedly it has played a major role in their success through millions of years of competition with other animals. These disguises worked in two ways—namely to protect the animal from predators, and to conceal them as predators of animals to be used as food. While it took millions of years for the beautifully colored and patterned domestic Felids to evolve, man has upset these natural selection processes so that their survival, for now, is no longer based on normal rules of nature.

Color variations in races of mammals have been brought about through elimination by predators of variants whose coloration did not match that of their habitats as well as that of the races that survived. Many travelers have commented on the effectiveness of the zebra's stripes, the tiger's stripes and the giraffe's blotches in making these animals almost invisible in the thin cover of their normal habitats, especially at dusk when attack by predators is most likely to occur. Travelers have described the eerie feeling when they took their eyes off such an animal momentarily to find that when they looked back again it had disappeared entirely.

Dr. Hugh B. Cott at Cambridge, England, has extensively researched the subject of protective coloration. Dr. Cott, a

Zebra

leading authority on animal camouflage, also authored the book, "Adaptive Coloration in Animals."

Consideration of the basic principles of protective coloration is important to an understanding of the color and design of the coats that domestic cats inherited from ancestral wildcats, as well as the colors and designs of coats of the big cats now in existence. Dr. Cott has analyzed the basic general principles of protective coloration and design of coat colors of many animals including Felids. Succinctly put, the visible form of an animal can only be recognized when it is exhibited by difference of color or tone, or of light and dark shades from the surroundings. With reduction of such difference, an animal becomes more difficult to recognize and, in the absence of any differences, it becomes unrecognizable.

It follows that there are four steps in effective camouflage, namely: (1) color resemblance - degree of agreement between the object and background against which it is seen; (2) obliterative shading - counter lightening and darkening which eliminates the appearance of roundness or relief; (3) disruptive coloration - superimposed pattern of color variations and tones which tend to blur the outline or real surface form and replace it with an apparent but unreal contour; (4) shadow elimination of form.

Dr. Cott gives examples of how color and pattern of Felids are related to their habitat. Thus, the snow leopard has long white fur and lives in the almost treeless highlands of central Asia. The vertical, tawny-orange stripes of the tiger blend with the parallel grass stems and reeds of the swamps and grassy plains where it lives. The cats of forested areas are marked with disruptive spotted or streaked patterns. This is especially true on the jaguar, where the yellow in its coat is broken with black spots that constitute an effective disguise in jungle foliage. Modifications of this coat color are found on the ocelot that lives exclusively in the forests of the Americas, and the clouded leopard that lives in the forests of Southeast Asia. The fishing cat, whose general ground color is gray disrupted by elongated dark spots and stripes, lives in waterside thickets where this coloration is undoubtedly disguising. And it is so for other cats—their coats blend with the terrain.

The colors of the wild ancestors of the domestic cat undoubtedly evolved on the basis of the foregoing principles. The predominant colorations of Felis catus are browns, grays and blacks. Most have stripes or spots of brown or black on a gray or brownish ground color, although some have uniformly shaded coats, as exemplified by their larger cousin, the lion, who lives on

Siberian Tigers (Kings Dominion)

sandy plains and rocky places with low scrub.

Protective coloration in most purebred cats is no longer evident because of man's influence in breeding, and because it is no longer a factor in their surviv-al. However, protective coloration is still much in evidence in household pets, strays and feral cats, where the tabby pattern is so frequent as well as an as-sortment of familiar bracelets, stripes, splotches and patches of coloration. A frequently encountered color design among household pets and strays is a white bib with white paws on a ground color of gray, yellow or black. These colors are a legacy from their wild ancestors where they contributed to their survival although it is difficult for me to see how the white bib and paws were very effective in that respect. My cat is so marked and it gives away her whereabouts at night when she is outside. These markings are not as essential to survival as they were to that of their forerunners.

Protective coloration and design is very evident in the world of cats, but is by no means limited to cats. It exists throughout the animal world and, in some cases, reaches an almost unbelievable degree of ingenuity.

Leopard

Atlas Lion

CHAPTER IV

Panleukopenia

A comprehensive discussion of the diseases of Felids is beyond the scope of this book. However, one disease of Felids has been so devastating and so entwined with humanity in the past that our discussion will be confined to this single disease. At the outset, it should be mentioned that modern medical science has provided a vaccine to prevent this dreaded disease, now known as panleukopenia.

Panleukopenia is a viral disease (Tortor felis). The history of panleukopenia is not generally known to cat fanciers and others associated with the big cats. Furthermore, confusion is compounded because of the multiplicity of names that have been used for this disease in the past. For example, the disease now known as panleukopenia has had the following names: cat disease, cat distemper, cat enteritis, cat diphtheria, cat cholera, cat typhoid, cat typhus, colibacilliosis, coli, epizootic enteritis, croupous enteritis, feline infectious enteritis, agranulocytosis, adenomeloenteritis and malignant panleucokopenia. The reason for so many names was the worldwide prevalence of the disease. Those treating or studying it picked a name which, to them, seemed to be most descriptive. The present name "panleukopenia" describes the most characteristic lesion, namely a marked drop in the white blood cell count - a finding that was probably not known to early researchers of the disease. Gastrointestinal lesions occur but they are more general in nature and characteristic of other viral diseases.

Panleukopenia often has occurred as an epizootic (analogous to an epidemic among humans), infecting and killing the entire kitten population of certain areas and spreading from continent to continent. Panleukopenia probably has been more devastating among cats than plague has been among humans. There are records of 109 epidemics of bubonic plague in the first 1,500 years following the birth of Christ. Included is the devastating Black Death of the 14th century (1348-1349), during which an estimated 25,000,000 people, or one-fourth of all the inhabitants of Europe perished. Throughout the ages, it has been estimated that hundred of millions of people have died of the plague which is still prevalent.

In the 16th and 17th centuries, it was generally accepted that cats and dogs were carriers of the plague. During these epidemics, these animals were killed by the thousands. Although cats can contract the plague, they are not currently regarded as an important factor in its spread. It seems likely that concurrent epidemics of the plague in humans and epizootics of panleukopenia in cats led to the belief that cats were the cause of the plague. This, rather than their alleged association with the occult, may have been a principal reason for their disfavor and persecution during the Middle Ages.

Prior to 1928, infectious feline enteritis (undoubtedly panleukopenia) was attributed to a number of species of bacteria. The consensus at that time was that the colon bacillus, **Escherichia coli**, was the causative agent. On June 23, 1928, E. Nicolas read a report by J. Verge and N. Cristaformi before the French Academy of Sciences in Paris, entitled, "La Gastro-Enterite Infectiense Des Chats. Est-Elle Due a Un Virus Filterable?". They concluded that a virus was responsible, a fact which has been confirmed by all subsequent researchers. Ten years later, further outstanding advances were made by two groups of American investigators, and the term "panleukopenia" was first used to describe this disease. These advances were summarized accurately in an address by Myron Arlein, D.V.M. of Angell Memorial Hospital, in Boston, Mass., before the Massachussetts Veterinary Association on October 23, 1940. In 1938, according to Dr. Arlein, Lawrence and Syverton, of the University of Rochester School of Medicine, described a highly contagious disease of cats that has since been realized to be identical with the disease previously called infectious feline enteritis. These medical researchers classified the disease as a specific viral infection characterized by marked changes in the heamatopietic system (pertaining to or affecting the formation of blood cells). This was a most dramatic finding in the annals of animal pathology.

Prior to this discovery, it was accepted, as the name implied, that the so-called feline enteritis was a specific disease of the digestive tract. Veterinary science failed to react to this challenge. However, the Rochester researchers continued their studies. They were joined by Hammon and Enders, of the the Harvard Medical School, who independently studied and described the same disease, and confirmed the findings of the Rochester group.

Hammon and Enders showed conclusively that in the Boston area they were not dealing with a bacterial intestinal infection but rather a specific viral infection which they termed "panleucopenia." This name obviously characterizes a disease of the blood cells and blood-forming organs. "Panleukopenia" is the modern spelling of the name first used by Hammon and Enders.

Panleukopenia is world-wide in its distribution. It occurs in all parts of the United States, in all breeds of cats and in all seasons, although it seems more prevalent during the cold, damp weather of early spring and late fall. This disease occurs in other members of the cat family, as was first shown by Silvie Torres at the Instituto de Biologie, Animal, Rio de Janiro, Brazil, in 1941. Early in 1940, in the Zoological Garden of Recife City, Brazil, nine of 15 wildcats died and Dr. Torres identified the infecting virus as the same one that causes panleukopenia in domestic cats. The ocelot, jaguarundi, margay and puma, among others, are also highly susceptible to this disease. The largest cats, such as the tiger, are believed to be more resistant to the disease, although in zoos, they are all vaccinated for panleukopenia.

Panleukopenia is highly contagious and spreads rapidly. Infection occurs by practically all routes, such as direct contact of healthy cats with infected cats, or by exposure to contaminated quarters, bedding or other articles that have been in contact with infected cats. There is evidence that fleas harbor the virus and that they definitely can spread it. The virus is found in the urine, feces, vomitus, nasal secretions and most tissues of infected or exposed cats. Thus the disease apparently can be spread by cats that harbor the virus during the incubation period.

The virus remains virulent at room temperature (50-85°F) for three months, and it was found to be viable after six days in decomposing organic matter. It has been repeatedly observed that a barn contaminated by infected cats retains the live virus for at least a year, even in the absence of cats. It can be destroyed by heating for one minute at boiling water temperature (212°F), or at 133° for 30 minutes. Panleukopenia virus is not affected by antibiotics.

The natural incubation period is from two to ten days, but usually is five to

seven days. There are no symptoms of the disease during the incubation period so the onset appears suddenly. Death may occur within 12 to 24 hours after
signs of illness are first noticed in the most severe cases. Duration in severe
cases seldom exceeds five to seven days. Fulminating panleukopenia usually
occurs in recently weaned kittens up to six months of age. A perfectly healthy-
appearing kitten may die within eight to 12 hours, an occurrence which leads
owners to suspect poisoning.

I once returned home from a cat show on a Sunday evening. We had three
little kittens about eight weeks old. On the following Thursday, all three
kittens came down with what appeared to be panleukopenia, and two of them
died within two days. After this experience, I always took my shoes off imme-
diately upon returning from cat shows and washed them with warm water
and soap. I also took a shower and changed my clothes before coming into
contact with any of our cats. I never had a similar experience after following
this procedure.

The mortality rate in kittens under six months of age is near 90 percent and
in older cats it is 50 to 60 percent.

Clinically, panleukopenia follows several courses. Some cases are mild,
asymptomatic and rarely recognized. Some cases are afebrile. In other cases,
the first symptom is a fever of 104-105° for the first 24 hours and a return to
normal temperature for the next 24 hours, followed by about three more days
of fever. Death may occur in the first febrile period with the temperature
becoming subnormal before death. Listlessness, prostration and loss of
appetite occur during the first 48 hours. The cat desires water but cannot
drink. Vomiting of a white or yellow froth may occur. Diarrhea may occur two
to four days after the initial temperature rise. The crisis occurs about seven
days after onset. The first sign of recovery, if it occurs, is to take a drink of
water and eat something. Once this happens, eventual recovery is fairly
certain and rapid. I had a mature cat that had panleukopenia. She stayed
under some bushes for about one week, then she came out, took a drink of
water and ate something. Her recovery was very rapid from this point. This
was in the days before the vaccine was developed.

The most striking lesion in panleukopenia is the decrease in the leucocyte
(white blood cell) count, either gradually or precipitously. The normal leucocyte count is about 15,000 per cubic centimeter. Lawrence and Syverton found
that the average count at the height of the disease was 1,350 per cc. Of 113
cats, 22 had counts of 0 to 200; 19 had counts above 3,000 and only one cat had
a count of 6,000. After the crisis, if the cat recovers, the leucocyte count
increases rapidly - 4,000 to 6,000 per day.

Treatment of cats with panleukopenia consists of careful sanitation, pro-
vision of warm, draft-free quarters, prevention of dehydration, supplying
electrolyte and nutrients and administration of a broad-spectrum antibiotic to
prevent secondary infection. Whole blood transfusions are the most important
treatment.

Strict isolation of the sick cat to prevent spread of the disease is important.
After recovery, or death, all litter should be burned, and the quarters cleaned
and disinfected. Susceptible kittens should not be brought into the house for
three or four months after a cat has had panleukopenia on the premises.

Temporary protection (passive immunity) from panleukopenia can be con-
ferred on susceptile cats and kittens by injection of immune serum (containing
antibodies); that is blood serum obtained from cats that have recovered from
panleukopenia. This antiserum is most effective if given one or two days before exposure, although it can also be effective when given up to three days
before onset of the symptoms, this is a few days after exposure. Normal feline
serum has some protective effect, but requires a larger dose because it contains
fewer antibodies than immune serum.

Another very effective vaccine that induces active immunity to panleukopenia is made from formalized suspension of liver, spleen and lymph nodes from cats killed at the height of the disease. Enders and Hammon first described this vaccine in 1940. The vaccine is given in two injections at intervals of seven to ten days. Immunity occurs about seven days after the second injection. A formalized vaccine prepared from minks suffering from a similar disease also imparts immunity to cats from panleukopenia. Immunity to panleukopenia using mink vaccine also occurs about seven days after the second injection.

Normally, kittens should be vaccinated upon weaning (seven to eight weeks), but if there is danger of exposure to panleukopenia, they should be vaccinated at four to five weeks of age and then revaccinated again after weaning.

The duration of immunity produced by these vaccines is not certain but veterinarians recommend that cats be given a single injection of vaccine each year.

Permanent immunity results from an attack of panleukopenia. Up to 40 percent of cats show a natural resistance to panleukopenia. Enders and Hammon showed that resistance to panleukopenia of naturally immune females is transferred to her kittens probably via the placenta. This observation provides a possible explanation why up to 40 percent of cats show a natural immunity to panleukopenia. The kittens of the immune mother may acquire a mild form of the disease and thus become actively immune for life.

Cat lovers all over the world owe a debt of gratitude to research scientists like Enders, Hammon, Lawrence, Syverton, Verge, Cristoformi and others whose pioneering studies brought the deadly and dreaded panleukopenia under control.

Bobcat

CHAPTER V

Photographs Of The Big Cats

A picture is said to be worth a thousand words. Many words have been used to describe the cat family. The following photographs of big cats allow you to form your own judgement as to the accuracy of the foregoing maxim.

ATLAS LION *(Panthera leo)*: The lion weighs from 400 to 500 pounds. The Atlas lion became extinct in its native North Africa in 1922. It survives only in captivity. The National Zoological Park in Washington, D.C., has several of them.

The Atlas lion differs from other lions in that the male has a long, thick, dark mane that extends along the back and shoulders, and a prominent belly-mane running in parallel strips the full length of the stomach. There are long tufts of hair on the elbows and tail. Its coat is thicker and grayish-tawny in contrast to reddish-yellow coats of the East African lions. The Atlas females look much the same as those of the other types of lions, except that they have longer tail tufts.

Lions are the only big cats with noticeable manes. Males have them, females do not. No one is sure what function the manes serve but several theories have been advanced: (1) the thick hairs of the mane protect the neck and throat from scratches and bites during fights with another male; (2) the mane shows the male's status and power. A heavy mane might impress a female and attract her, or it might be a symbol of strength to another male and intimidate him; (3) the mane serves to distinguish one male lion from another. The manes range from black to yellow and from sparse to heavy. These variations might enable one lion to recognize another at a safe distance and thus prevent a violent encounter.

Lion (Kings Dominion)

25

Lioness (Kings Dominion)

Lions, unlike other cats, group together to live, hunt and rear their young. These groups, called "prides," can include anywhere from just a few animals to up to 30 or more. Atlas lions are not considered pride lions. They travel alone, in pairs or as mother and cubs. The pride is composed of two to four males, the females, and their young. The females form the stable nucleus of the pride. All are related—mothers, daughters, aunts and nieces—and remain together for life. Adult males are temporary members of the family, they stay for a few months or a few years before leaving or being forcibly replaced by a new male. When young males reach an age of 3½ years, they leave the pride to wander alone. They may join another pride or remain as nomads for the rest of their lives. This social behavior, while hard on the males, prevents inbreeding. Although each mother is primarily responsible for her own young, other females sometimes help in caring for the cubs. This communal life prepares the young female for her own motherhood. Males, however, play no part in this. Growing up within the pride, the cubs learn the necessary skills of hunting.

Lions use complex gestures, postures, facial expressions, and sounds to establish relationships within the pride. When separated from the pride, they keep in touch by scent marking and roaring. The life span of the lion in the wild is 15 to 30 years.

The natural diet of lions consists of both carrion and fresh meat. Lions are predators of large animals such as wildebeests, antelope, zebra, buffalo, and the like. The prey that they kill provides a lot of meat at one time so that lions need to hunt less often than they would if their prey were smaller. Consequently, a lion's digestive system is adapted to "feast or famine." The lion can gorge itself on up to 60 pounds of meat, or one-fourth of its body weight in one night. During the next couple of days, the lion lies around and rests for 20 hours a day, eating and digesting its large feast.

26

The gestation period of members of the genus Panthera ranges from 92 to 113 days. The young number anywhere from one to six, usually two or three.

The Atlas lion lived from northern Lybia to Morocco. Lions once inhabited Europe, Asia Minor, India and Africa. Now, most live in East Africa in areas such as the Sarengeti plains of Tanzania. These open plains, with tall grasses and shady acacia trees are an ideal environment for the lion. These plains are home to vast herds of hoofed mammals, the lion's primary prey. During the rainy season, prey is plentiful because the herds of wildebeest, zebra, gazelle, and eland leave the woodlands to eat the new grasses of the plains. During the dry season, the woodland animals leave the plains making prey less abundant. Then, the lion's choice of food is limited to such animals as impala and cape buffalo. The lion's habitat is rapidly decreasing as open land is cultivated and over-grazed by domestic stock. The lion's best chance of survival is in the protected areas such as Sarengeti National Park and the Masai Mara Reserve.

Atlas Lion

Atlas Lion

Atlas Lion

Bengal Tiger

Bengal Tigers

BENGAL TIGER *(Panthera tigris)*: The Bengal tiger weighs from 500 to 600 pounds. Tigers come in two basic colors: yellow with black stripes, and white with dark brown or black stripes. The tiger is a solitary animal; it travels alone, except during the mating season or when a nursing mother and her young cubs travel together. The stripes of the tiger are one of the great examples of natural camouflage. Against a plain background, the tiger pattern of yellow with black stripes stands out vividly. But, in its jungle or reedy habitat, the stripes help the tiger to blend with the background. This excellent disguise helps the tiger to sneak stealthily on its prey. In contrast, the lion hunts in open grasslands so its solid brownish-yellow coat blends with the surroundings. The lion would be as poorly disguised in the tiger's habitat as the tiger would be in the lion's habitat. Tigers inhabiting an area are always aware of each other's presence. They communicate by scent and sound. A traveling tiger marks its trail by spraying on trees, scratching trees, and scraping up small piles of soil and leaves. They also make their presence known by roaring.

Bengal Tiger

White Tiger and Cubs

The line of white tigers that exists in zoos today was begun by the Mararajah of Reva in India. For many years, there had been reports of wild white tigers in the forests of Reva. In 1951, the Mararajah captured a young white male and bred it with an ordinary yellow female. Several yellow cubs resulted, but when the white male was mated with one of these grown cubs, several white cubs were born. These white tigers then are the ancestors of the white tigers now fairly common in zoos all over the world. The first white tiger in the United States was purchased for $10,000. She was brought from India to the National Zoological Park in 1960, by Dr. Theodore H. Reed, director of this zoo since 1958. This tiger's name was Mohini. Mohini was the mother of several white cubs. White tigers are not albinos. Nor are they a different species from the yellow tiger. The white tiger is a genetic oddity, produced by a rare combination of mutated (changed) genes. Unlike true albinos, the white tigers have some dark fur; colored brown stripes on a white background. They also have blue eyes, pink noses and pink paw pads.

Bengal Tigers

Bengal Tiger

Bengal Tigers (Tiger By The Tail)

Tigers are great swimmers and spend much time wading in swamps. The life span of the tiger is from 12 to 19 years.

The natural diet of the tiger consists of any animal they can kill. Included, are sambar (deer), barking deer, wild pigs, crocodiles, turtle, fish and even leopards, and on occasion, other tigers. Tigers usually stalk their prey with a silent, stealthy crawl until they are within charging distance.

Tigers have three to four young after a gestation period of 92 to 113 days. The mother cares for the cubs until they are old enough to hunt for themselves.

The tiger is found sparingly in China but is more common to the jungles of India south of the Himalayan mountains, southern China and the Malayan peninsula. The Siberian tiger lives in the cold forests of Manchuria and Siberia. Their preferred habitat, however, is the tropical jungles and swampy areas.

White Tiger

White Tiger and Cubs

Bengal Tigers

White Tiger and Cub

Leopard

Leopard

LEOPARD *(Panthera pardus)*: The leopard weighs up to 200 pounds. The leopard, like the jaguar, has a cinnamon-buff coloration with a rosette pattern. It also comes in a black version. The leopard is quieter and more cunning than the lion or the tiger. Also, unlike these two big cats, the leopard is a tree climber. It often attacks its prey by springing from an overhanging bough. All of the big cats are very powerful, but the leopard is especially so. As an example of this strength, a single part of a buffalo weighing 99 pounds was found in an acacia tree about 10 feet above the ground where it had been placed by a leopard. Leopards usually travel alone at night, or in pairs or family groups of four to six.

The natural diet of the leopard consists of almost any animal it can over-power including hoofstock, monkeys, small mammals, fish and occasionally fruit.

The leopard breeds throughout the year, and has from two to four young.

The leopard is the most widely distributed of any of the wild Felids. It is found in most of Asia and Africa. Likewise, it inhabits a great variety of regions—from tropical forests and rocky areas with dense or sparse vegetation to the cold highlands of the Himalayas. In rocky regions, the leopard lives in caves, while in forested regions it lives in dense vegetation.

Leopard

39

Cheetah

CHEETAH *(Acinonyx jubatus)*: The cheetah weighs from 100 to 140 pounds. The ground coloration of the upper body is tawny to pale buff or grayish white and the underside of the body is white. There is a black stripe from the eye to the mouth on each side. The coat pattern consists of solid black spots set close together over the entire body. It is a rangy Felid with extremely long legs, round head and short ears. The pupils of the eyes when contracted are round in contrast with the slits of the domestic cat. The cheetah is the swiftest of the mammals. Its long legs and lithe body enable the cheetah to reach a speed of up to 70 miles an hour for a short distance. They catch their prey with these terrific bursts of speed after stalking it as far as possible, sometimes chasing it

Cheetah

for up to four miles (at speeds of less than 70 miles an hour). They have regular scratching posts, a fact which often leads to their capture by an alert hunter who sets nooses at the posts. Cheetahs hunt in daylight by sight rather than scent. They sometimes hunt on bright, moonlight nights. They travel alone or in small groups. They can purr like a domestic cat, and can utter birdlike chirps when alarmed or when eating. They also have a wild cry which is similar to a barking howl.

The natural diet of the cheetah consists of small antelopes and other small animals, as well as birds.

The cheetah has two to four young after a gestation period of 84 to 95 days.

The cheetah lives in India westward to Egypt, Libya and Morocco. It also lives in tropical Africa from Nigeria, Sudan and Somaliland south to southern Africa. While they prefer open country, they also live in denser savannahs (plains with sparse trees and coarse grasses bordering on the tropics).

Jaguar

JAGUAR *(Panthera onca)*: The jaguar weighs from 150 to 300 pounds. Its coloration is cinnamon-buff patterned accompanied by rosettes with small black spots in their centers. The leopard has a similar pattern but does not have spots in the center of the rosettes. Its South American Indian name is "jaguara," which is said to mean, "animal that overcomes its prey in a single bound."

The natural diet of the jaguar consists of peccaries (wild pigs), capybaras (large guinea pig-like aquatic animals), turtles, fish and other small mammals, and unfortunately, domestic livestock which makes them vulnerable to hunting.

The jaguar has a gestation period of 100 to 110 days, after which one to three young are born.

The jaguar ranges from southwestern United States southward to Argentina. It lives in thick woods and dry scrub lands.

Jaguar

Jaguar

Puma

Puma

Puma

Puma

PUMA *(Felis concolor)*: The puma weighs from 80 to 230 pounds. It is also known as cougar and mountain lion. Their coloration is yellowish-brown on the back to whitish underneath. Young pumas have dark brown spots and ringed tails, but these markings disappear as the animals become one-half grown. Except for the jaguarundi, the puma is the only unmarked Felid in the Americas. The life span of the puma is up to 23 years.

The natural diet of the puma consists of a variety of wild animals and, unfortunately, domestic livestock which marks them for killing by ranchers.

The gestation period of the puma is 90 to 96 days. The litter size for this genus is anywhere from one to six, usually two to four. The mother stays with the young until they are able to hunt for themselves.

The puma has the most extensive range of any native animal in the Americas. It ranges from British Columbia in Canada, to Patagonia in Argentina.

Bobcat

BOBCAT *(Lynx rufus)*:
Bobcats weigh from 12
to 25 pounds, somewhat
more than the domestic cat.
The genus Lynx includes,
obviously, lynxes, bobcats,
wildcats and caracals. The
coloration of the bobcat is
generally pale brown to
reddish-brown streaked
with blackish or dark spots
and a white underbelly.
They have smaller ear tufts
than the lynx. They usually
travel alone, although
groups numbering several
individuals have been re-
ported. They are expert tree
climbers, swimmers and
powerful fighters, using both
tooth and claw as weapons.
They are mostly nocturnal,
hunting by sight and smell
over an irregular route of up
to 25 miles in one night.
Their life span is from 10 to
20 years.

Bobcat

The natural diet of the bobcat consists of any small mammals or birds that
it can kill.

Mating takes place in late winter. The gestation period is about 60 days, like
the domestic cat (63 days). One to four young are born in natural shelters, in
thickets, or rocky terrain. The young weigh about 340 grams (a little more than
one-half pound) at birth. Their eyes open in nine to ten days. They are weaned
at about two months and the females can breed again after one year. The family stays together for six to nine months.

The bobcat ranges over southern Canada, the United States (except the
midwest cornbelt), and southward into Mexico.

Serval

SERVAL *(Felis serval)*: The serval is a long-legged, short-tailed, large-eared Felid of slender build—sort of a small-scaled cheetah. The ground color is yellowish-brown on the back shading to almost white on the underside, with black or dark brown spots. Like the cheetah, the serval has great speed for short distances and in high grass, moves by long, high leaps. The serval is a fierce fighter and has been known to kill dogs.

The natural diet of the serval consists of rodents, other small mammals, birds and fish. It often catches birds that have taken flight or on perches 10 feet above the ground. The serval is a skillful climber who can catch hyraxes in trees. It hunts alone, more during the day than most small cats.

The serval has from one to four young. Servals come together to mate but do not have a definite breeding season.

The serval is found in Africa.

CLOUDED LEOP-ARD *(Neofelis nebulosa)*: The clouded leopard weighs from 35 to 50 pounds. Adult clouded leopards have a grayish or yellowish ground color with black markings in the form of circles, ovals, rectangles and rosettes. Young animals lack these markings. This is a rather long animal with short heavy legs and broad paws. The clouded leopard, like that of its larger cousin (leopard), hunts in trees and springs on its prey on the ground, although it also hunts on the ground. Many of

Clouded Leopard

the clouded leopards in captivity are gentle, playful and like to be petted by their keepers. Some play by the hour with small articles in their cages, while others prefer to sleep.

The natural diet of the clouded leopard consists of a variety of animals, including monkeys, birds, pigs, deer, young buffalo, porcupines, and, unfortunately, cattle and goats. It is not known to attack people.

The gestation period is not known. It usually gives birth to two young in a hollow tree.

The clouded leopard inhabits Nepal and Sikkim, eastward to southern China, Hainan, Taiwan and southward to Sumatra, Malayan States and Borneo. It lives in jungles, shrub, and swampy areas.

LEOPARD CAT *(Felis bengalensis)*: The leopard cat is about the same size as the domestic cat and thus its weight falls roughly in the range of five to 15 pounds. The coloration is a light ground color with black spots. It is generally considered to be nocturnal. It is usually seen in pairs or in small family groups.

The natural diet of the leopard cat is small mammals, small amphibians and reptiles.

The leopard cat has from one to four young.

The leopard cat lives in eastern Asia and the Philippine Islands. Its habitat is hilly country with dense forests and grasslands.

Leopard Cat

Asian Elephant

CHAPTER VI

Photographs Of Nonfeline Mammals

Nonfeline mammals are not as photogenic as are felines, in my opinion. Nevertheless, most of them are very appealing in photographs. The objective of this chapter is to capture the beauty and dignity of nonfeline mammals. These qualities are as apparent with these animals, but in different ways, as they are with the Felids.

ELEPHANTS: The African elephant is the largest land mammal, weighing up to 7.7 tons. The largest mammal in the world is the whale, which weighs up to 150 tons or about eleven times the weight of the African elephant. The whale requires water to support its huge body. All of the largest land mammals, including the elephant, are herbivorous.

During the Pleistocene epoch (last million years), elephants roamed every continent except Australia. The Proboscides consisted of six families, only one of which still exists. The African and Asian elephants comprise the family of existing elephants. The African elephant is the larger of the two.

The comparative heights and weights of the elephant, hippopotamus, rhinoceros and whale are shown in the following table.

African Elephant

African Elephant

Table 6.1
**Comparative Sizes of Elephant, Hippopotamus
Rhinoceros and Whale**

	Height (feet)	*Weight (tons)*
African elephant	13.1	7.7
Asian elephant	9.8	5.5
Hippopotamus, Nile	4.9	5.0
Hippopotamus, Pygmy	3.3	0.25
Rhinoceros	6.6	4.4
Whale		150.0

Since the elephant is so large, it requires a great amount of food. It can eat about 250 pounds of food a day, and spends up to 18 hours a day eating and searching for food.

In their constant search for food, elephants are destroying their own habitats, now mostly on preserves. They reach high with their trunks to browse on leaves and twigs. They often knock down trees to obtain food beyond reach, even eating bark and roots. A savannah that was lightly forested becomes strewn with stripped and upended trees. Soon, grasslands replace the savannah and the elephants have created an unsuitable habitat for themselves. Park naturalists are aware of this problem and keep elephant populations thinned in effort to lessen habitat destruction. Yet another animal is confined to a constantly decreasing area due to expansion of agriculture and human civilization.

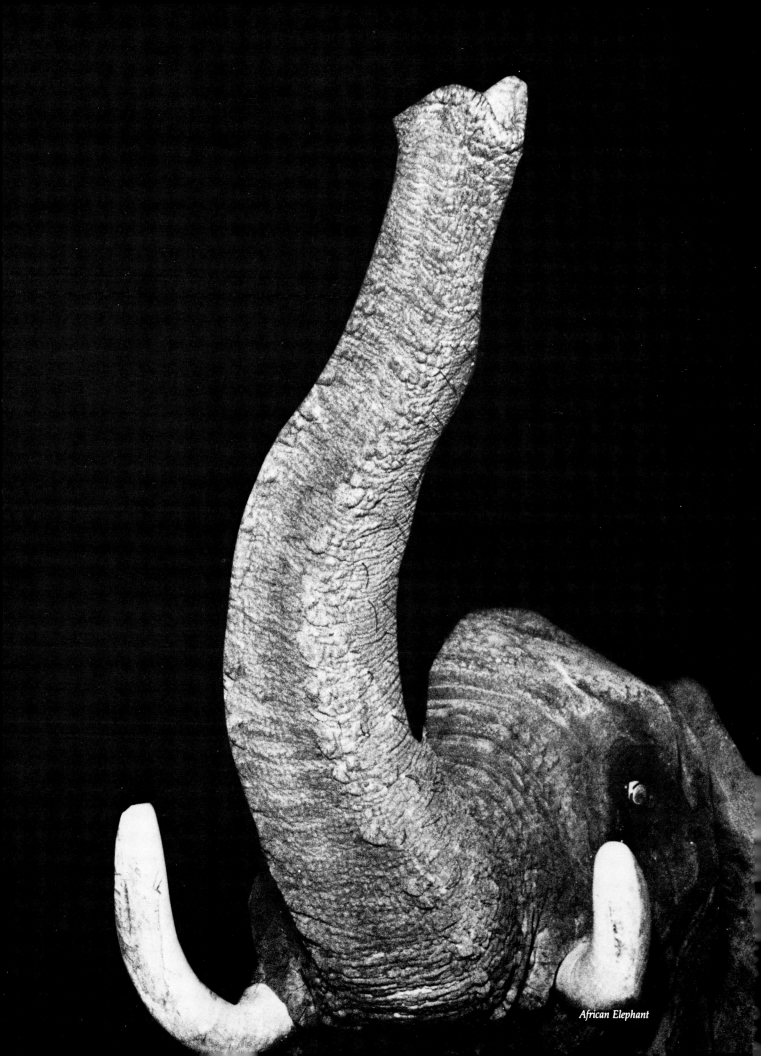

African Elephant

AFRICAN ELEPHANT *(Loxodonta africana)*: The African elephant weighs from 5.5 to about 8 tons, and stands 10 to 13 feet tall at the shoulder. It is the largest terrestrial mammal. The dull, brownish-gray skin is covered with sparse, black, bristly hairs. The most conspicuous external feature of the elephant is the trunk, which has a finger-like projection at its end enabling it to pick up small objects. The ears are huge, ranging up to 5 feet from top to bottom. The ears are part of the cooling system of the elephant. The largest male tusk recorded was over 11 feet long and weighed 235 pounds. Tusks of the female are smaller, weighing only about 40 pounds. These tusks are prized as sources of ivory, used in making numerous articles of commerce. This has led to the destruction of a large number of elephants by hunters, often illegally. African elephants live in herds consisting of both sexes and all ages, which are usually led by an old cow. Old males sometimes remain solitary for life. Members of the herd will assist a wounded comrade by walking on either side to prevent it from falling. Elephants are intelligent and tame easily. While African elephants are not now used much as beasts of burden, they have been so used in the past. Water is sucked up in the trunk and blown out into the mouth. They spray their backs and other objects. The life span of the elephant is about that of man—50 to 70 years.

The natural diet of the elephant consists of grasses, tree branches, leaves, fruit, bark, roots and pithy wood.

The gestation period is about 22 months. One young is born, usually in July or August. The herd waits about two days after birth until the infant has sufficient strength to accompany them. A female may bear four to five young in her lifetime.

The African elephant ranges in most parts of central, eastern, and southern Africa. It prefers a variety of habitats, such as savannahs, river valleys, thornbush, dense forests, desert and scrub lands.

Asian Elephant

ASIAN ELEPHANT *(Elephas maximus)*: The Asian elephant weighs up to 5.5 tons and stands up to 10 feet at the shoulder. The coloration is dark gray to brown. The hair covering is long, bristly and scant. The trunk of the Asiatic elephant has two finger-like projections at the tip in contrast to one on the African elephant. A more noticeable difference is that the ears of the Asian are much smaller than those of the African elephant. Asian elephants travel and live in herds of 15 to 30 individuals, usually led by a female. Members of the herd consist of females, the young and one old bull. They are peaceable when left alone, although occasionally some individuals are dangerous. Females have two nipples just behind the front legs. The young nurse with their mouths. The testes of the male remain in the abdomen. Their life span is 50 to 70 years.

Asian Elephant

They have been domesticated for centuries, and are intelligent and docile when well treated. They are used as draft animals, for transportation, and for hunting. The greatest enemy of the elephant is the tiger.

The natural diet of the Asian elephant consists of grasses, vines, leaves, tender shoots and fruit.

The Asiatic elephant has no regular breeding season. The gestation period is 607 to 641 days, and usually one young is born with occasional twins. The weight of the baby is about 200 pounds. Maximum physical growth is attained in 25 years and sexual maturity is reached in eight to 12 years.

The range of the Asian elephant is India, Assam, Burma, Thailand, the Malay States, Sumatra, and Sri Lanka. A few are found in Borneo. It is thought that they were imported here a few centuries ago. They prefer a variety of habitats, from thick jungle areas to open grassy plains.

Asian Elephant

Nile Hippopotamus

Hippopotamus (Kings Dominion)

Hippopotamus (Kings Dominion)

HIPPOPOTAMUS *(Hippopoma amphibius)*: The hippopotamus stands 5 feet tall at the shoulder and weighs from 3 to 5 tons. The coloration ranges from a slate-copper-brown shading to dark brown above and purplish underneath. While they appear to be hairless, they are scantily covered with short, fine hairs. Hippopotamuses spend most of their time in water. When submerged, they close their nostrils and ears. They can see and breath without exposing themselves because their eyes and nostrils protrude while the rest of the body is submerged. They can tolerate salt water as well as fresh water. They travel more than a quarter of a mile from water at night in search of food. They travel alone (usually old bulls), in pairs or in small groups of six although the group may number up to 20 or 30. The life span is from 40 to 50 years.

The natural diet consists mainly of grasses adjacent to water's edge. Occasionally, they do extensive damage to planted crops by trampling and eating.

Hippopotamuses seem to breed at all times of the year. One calf (rarely two) is born after a gestation period of 227 to 240 days. The young are born under water and they also nurse under water. The calf weighs from 60 to 100 pounds. In captivity, both sexes mature at three years of age.

Hippopotamuses at one time ranged over all of Africa but now are confined to areas south of 17 degrees north latitude. Their preferred habitat is rivers with adjacent marshes of reeds, and grasslands.

Hippopotamuses (Kings Dominion)

Nile Hippopotamuses

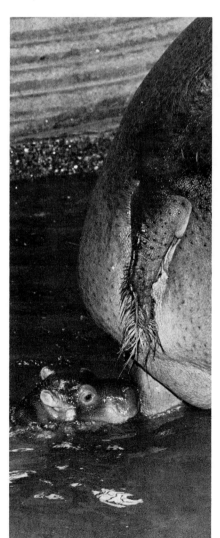

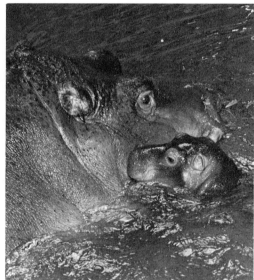

Nile Hippopotamuses

Nile Hippopotamuses

White Rhinoceros (Kings Dominion)

Rhino

WHITE RHINOC-EROS *(Ceratotherium simum)*: The shoulder height of the White Rhinoceros may reach a little over 6 feet, and their weight up to 5 tons. The rhinoceros is a little taller than the hippopotamus but their maximum weights are about the same. The rhinoceros has a slight size advantage because it is the largest living land mammal next to the

Rhinoceroses

elephant. Their coloration is slate gray to yellowish-brown. It is hairless except for ear tufts and tail bristles. Most rhinoceroses have two horns—the Indian one-horned rhinoceros is either extinct or nearly so. Their horns are made up of keratinous material, not bone. The white rhinoceros is more sociable than the black one. They are normally timid, but are ferocious when held at bay. They live in pairs, and family groups of three or four are common. In good feeding areas, groups can be a large as six or seven. They are active during the evening, night, and early morning. They rest during the day and are fond of wallowing in muddy pools and sandy river beds. They are often accompanied by tick birds and egrets, who ride on their backs and act as sentinels. The mutual benefit to the birds is feeding on parasites and insects stirred up as the rhinoceros walks through the grass. The black rhinoceros can run at a speed of 30 miles an hour for short distances. Their life span is 50 years. The natural diet

Rhinoceros & Goat

Rhinoceros

of the rhinoceros consists of leaves, twigs, shrubs and various fruits.

Rhinoceroses appear to breed throughout the year. During the mating season, a pair may stay together for four months. They breed every several years. A single young is born after a gestation period of 17 to 19 months. Females become sexually mature at four to five years of age. A female offspring, weighing 110 pounds at birth, gained about 880 pounds (total weight, 990 pounds) in 18 months. The offspring becomes active soon after birth and remains with its mother until another young one is born.

The Asiatic two-horned rhinoceros was found in Assam, Burma, Thailand, Malayan States and Borneo. The two-horned white rhinoceros lives in southern Africa, mostly on game preserves. Their preferred habitat is savannah and bushy areas.

Rhinoceroses

Ouch!

En Garde

Touché

Rhinoceros & Goat

Kodiak Bears

Kodiak Bear

Kodiak Bear

KODIAK BEAR *(Ursus arctos)*: The Kodiak, or Alaskan Brown bear is the largest living carnivore. They weigh up to 1,700 pounds. The coloration is usually dark brown, but colors range from cream to almost black. These bears will not normally attack a human unless it is attacked first or if its young is threatened. Their eyesight is very poor and they will usually run on sight of a human. The strength of these bears is tremendous. Adults do not climb trees. During the winter, they hibernate in natural shelters such as caves or dens which they dig for themselves. They travel alone, except during the mating season. Females and cubs travel together and groups form at food sources. The life span of the bear is from 15 to 34 years.

Cubs are born during the winter hibernation. The gestation period is from 180 to 250 days. A cub weighs about one pound at birth but gains almost 200 pounds during the first year of its life. The mother cares for the cubs for at least one year. Females breed at about three years of age.

The natural diet of the Kodiak bear consists of plants, vegetables, fish, and other flesh. They are not fast enough to prey on hoofed stock, except for the bison. Unfortunately, they sometimes kill domestic livestock.

Kodiak bears inhabit the Alaskan peninsula, Kodiak Island, and several other artic islands in southeast Alaska. Their habitat is in forests and open land near the sea.

Kodiak Bear

Kodiak Bear

Kodiak Bears

Kodiak Bear

Polar Bear

POLAR BEAR *(Thalarctos maritimus):* The maximum weight of the polar bear is 1,600 pounds, but the average weight is 900 pounds for males and 700 pounds for females. Their coloration is white to creamy-white throughout the year. The neck is long with a relatively small head. The soles of the feet are covered with hair, which contributes to good traction on the ice and insulation against arctic cold. The polar bear is a great traveler, sometimes wandering great distances on land and also at sea on ice floes. They can run much faster then their bulk would indicate. They can outrun a reindeer over a short distance. They can also swim great distances, reaching speeds of up to four miles an hour in the water. They travel alone except during mating season; females travel with their cubs. Polar bears do not hibernate like other bears. Their life span is 34 years.

Females have from one to four young. The gestation period is about nine months. Pregnant females dig a den in the snow and appear to hibernate until the young are born. The mother spends the winter sleeping and nursing her young on fat-rich milk. By March or April, the mother begins to break out of the den. Her cubs, which weighed about two pounds at birth, now weigh about 20 pounds. The cubs stay with the mother for one to two years. They start breeding at 2½ to four years of age, and breed every other year.

Polar bears eat seals, fish, birds, reindeer, musk oxen, rabbits, carrion and plant materials.

The polar bear lives in the arctic regions around the north pole, the coasts of Alaska, Canada and the Soviet Union. The habitat is snowy tundra and drifting ice floes in open water.

Polar Bear

Polar Bear

Sloth Bear

Sloth Bears

Sloth Bears

SLOTH BEAR *(Melursus ursinus)*: The sloth bear weighs from 200 to 250 pounds. The basic black coloration consists of various mixtures of brown and gray, as well as cinnamon and red. The characteristic mark on the chest is typically shaped as a V or Y and ranges from white to yellow or chestnut-brown. Sloth bears do not hibernate and are mainly nocturnal. Like most bears, their sight, and in this case hearing, is poorly developed but the sense of smell is fairly keen. Under normal conditions, the sloth bear is nonaggressive toward humans, but because their sight is so poor, they may inadvertently come close to a human, causing them to panic, rush and maul the person. Consequently, they are held in respect by the natives. Their life span in captivity is about 40 years.

Breeding usually occurs in June in India, and throughout the year in Sri Lanka. The gestation period is about seven months. One or two cubs, rarely three, are born in a den. In two or three months, the cubs come out of the den and often ride on the mother's back. They remain with their mother for two or three years, or until almost fully grown. They are monogamous and both parents care for the young.

Sloth bears live on insects, grubs, honey, eggs, plant material and carrion.

The sloth bear lives in the forests of India and Sri Lanka.

75

Spectacled Bear

SPECTACLED BEAR *(Tremarctos ornatus)*: The spectacled bear weighs up to 300 pounds. The body coloration is uniformly black or brownish-black, except for large white circles or semi-circles around the eyes, and a white semi-circle on the lower part of the neck from which white lines extend onto the chest. These markings are variable and are completely lacking in some animals.

Spectacled bears have from one to three cubs. They travel alone except during mating season. Females and cubs travel together.

The natural diet is leaves, fruit and roots. Although reportedly the most herbivorous of all bears, in the wild, they prey on deer, guanacoes and vicunas.

The spectacled bear is a South American bear that inhabits western Venezuela, Columbia, Ecuador, Peru, and western Bolivia. They are mainly forest animals, but range into lower savannah and scrub lands.

Giant Panda

Giant Panda

GIANT PANDA

(Ailuropoda melanoleuca): The giant panda weighs from 165 to 350 pounds. The coat of the panda is thick and wooly. The coloration is black (sometimes with a brownish tinge) and white or reddish. The eye patches, ears, legs and body band are black. The teddy-bear appearance of the giant panda makes them a favorite among zoo visitors. Although the giant panda looks like a bear, it is considered to be more closely related to the raccoon (Procyonidae). Giant pandas live alone except during the breeding season and when with their young. They do not hibernate. If pursued by dogs, they climb trees but they prefer to spend most of their time on the ground.

The breeding season is during the spring, and one or two cubs are usually born in January. Sexual maturity is reached between four and ten years. They are very difficult to breed in captivity.

The principal component of their natural diet is bamboo stalks. They also feed on other plants and even animals. Occasionally, they catch fish and small rodents. Shortages of bamboo, which occur periodically, cause some losses by starvation in the wild.

Giant pandas live in central China, northern and central Szechnan province and south Kansu province. They live in dense forests high in the mountains. They live mainly on the ground with shelters in hollow trees, rock crevices and caves.

Giant Panda

Giant Panda

Lesser Panda

LESSER PANDA *(Ailurus fulgens)*: The lesser panda weighs from seven to ten pounds. It has a long, silky coat with a bushy tail. The coloration of the upper body is rusty to deep chestnut and is darkest along the middle of the back. The back of the ears, legs and underparts are dark reddish-brown or black. The tail is bushy and faintly ringed. The lesser panda is mostly nocturnal, sleeping during the day in trees. It is docile and when captured, does not struggle or fight. It tames readily, and is gentle, curious and quiet. Its usual call is a series of short whistles or squeals, but when provoked, it utters hisses or a series of snorts. They usually travel in pairs or family groups.

The lesser panda has one or two young; occasionally up to four young. The gestation period is 90 to 150 days; the irregularity is due to the fact that there is sometimes a delay in implantation. The young are blind from 21 to 30 days and are, therefore, highly dependent on their mother. They stay with their parents for about a year, or until the next litter is born.

The natural diet of the lesser panda consists of bamboo sprouts, grass, roots, fruit and acorns. They also occasionally eat eggs, and even birds and mice. However, they rarely eat meat

Lesser pandas live in the Yunnan and Szechnan provinces of China, Burma, Sikkim and Nepal in India. Their preferred habitat is bamboo forests at higher elevations. They prefer a colder climate than the giant panda.

Hyena

Hyenas

SPOTTED OR LAUGHING HYENA *(Crocuta crocuta)*: The hyena weighs from 130 to 180 pounds. The ground coloration is yellowish-gray, and the body spots are dark brown to black. The jaws of the hyena are probably the most powerful of any mammal in proportion to its size. This is the largest member of the hyena family. The hyena is capable of a running speed of up to 40 miles an hour. Hyenas are nocturnal. They form packs and are quite noisy. When in presence of food, they utter a characteristic howl. They get the name "laughing hyena" from a laugh-like sound uttered during the mating season or when otherwise excited. They have a life span of 25 years.

Female hyenas do not have a breeding season but have a cycle of 14 days throughout the year. The gestation period is 110 days. The number of young is one or two.

Hyenas are scavengers who eat carrion and small mammals. Unfortunately, they have also been known to kill domesticated animals, as well as sleeping children and adults. They have powerful necks and jaws, and can easily carry off a human body. Tribes in northern and central Africa left their dead from battles for the hyenas to eat. Hyenas also eat large numbers of locusts that plague the countryside from time to time.

Hyenas live in most of Africa south of the Sahara Desert. They live in holes, caves or lairs in dense vegetation.

Hyenas

82

Hyena

Timber Wolves

Timber Wolves

TIMBER WOLF *(Canis lupus)*: The adult timber wolf weighs up to 165 pounds. The basic ground color ranges from light gray to dark gray-brown. They are lithe and muscular with a deep chest, long, slender legs and bushy tail. Timber wolves live in packs consisting of family groups that may number up to 30 individuals. They are active both by day and by night. Their life span is 10 to 18 years in the wild. Wolves have been unjustly stigmatized with an undeserved evil relationship with man. These beliefs have been shown to be false, yet the prejudice remains. I wish to add my voice to that of others who are trying to dispel this myth.

Females usually have one litter (sometimes two) a year. The number of young varies from two to 13. The gestation period of most members of this family ranges from 49 to 79 days, with an av-

Timber Wolf

Timber Wolf

Timber Wolf

erage of 63 days. They are cared for by their mothers until they are strong enough to outrun their enemies.

The natural diet consists of deer, elk, moose, rabbit, mice, fish and carrion. They hunt the large hoofed animals in packs, using a relay system to tire their prey before the kill. They hunt the smaller prey as singles.

The range of the timber wolf includes western Canada, northern Minnesota and Michigan, and much of Europe and Asia. Their habitat consists of forests, steepes and mountains. They live in burrows, caves, crevices and hollow trees.

Continued on page 139

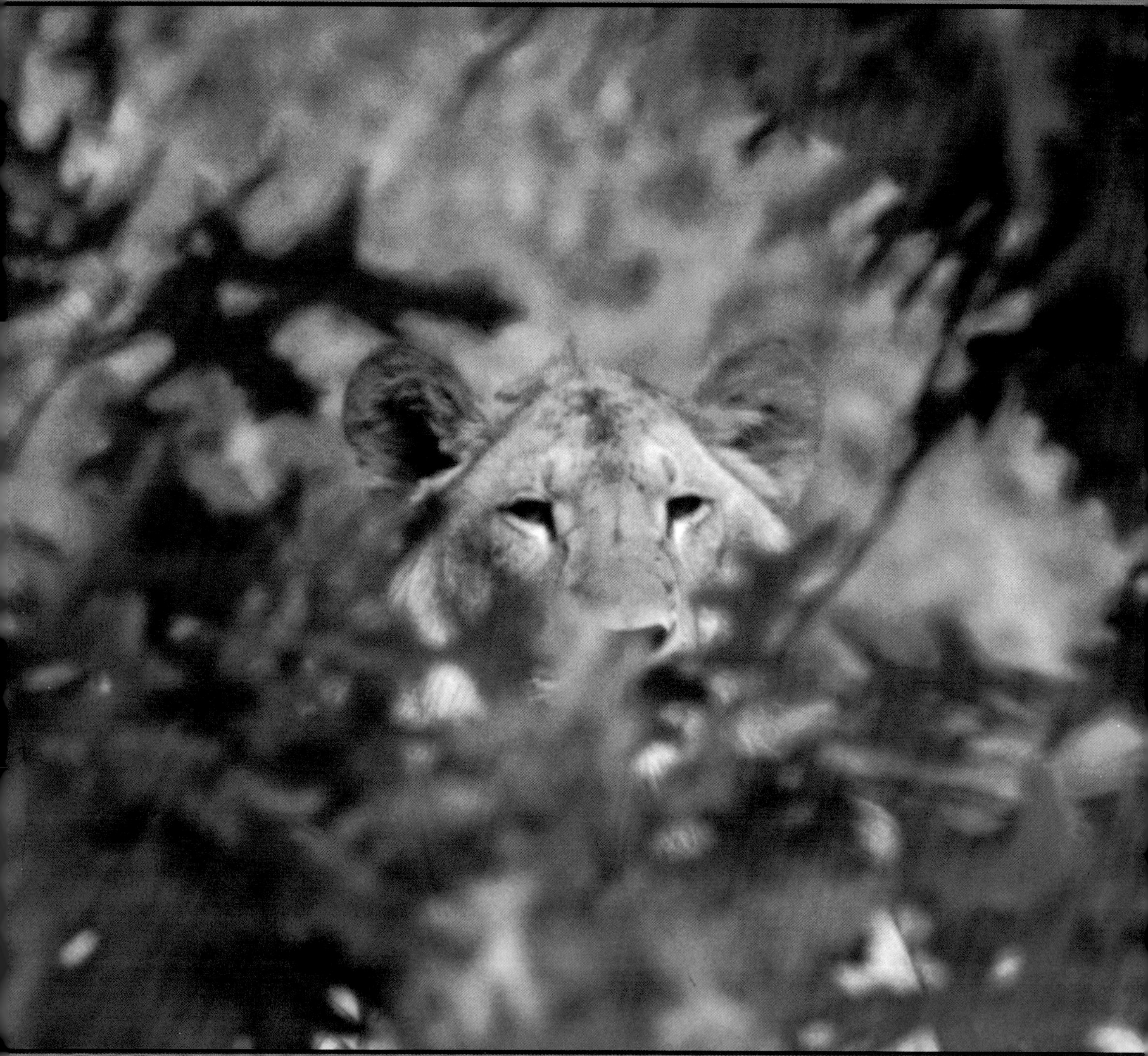

Leopard

Polar Bear

Churchill, Manitoba

Kodiak Bear

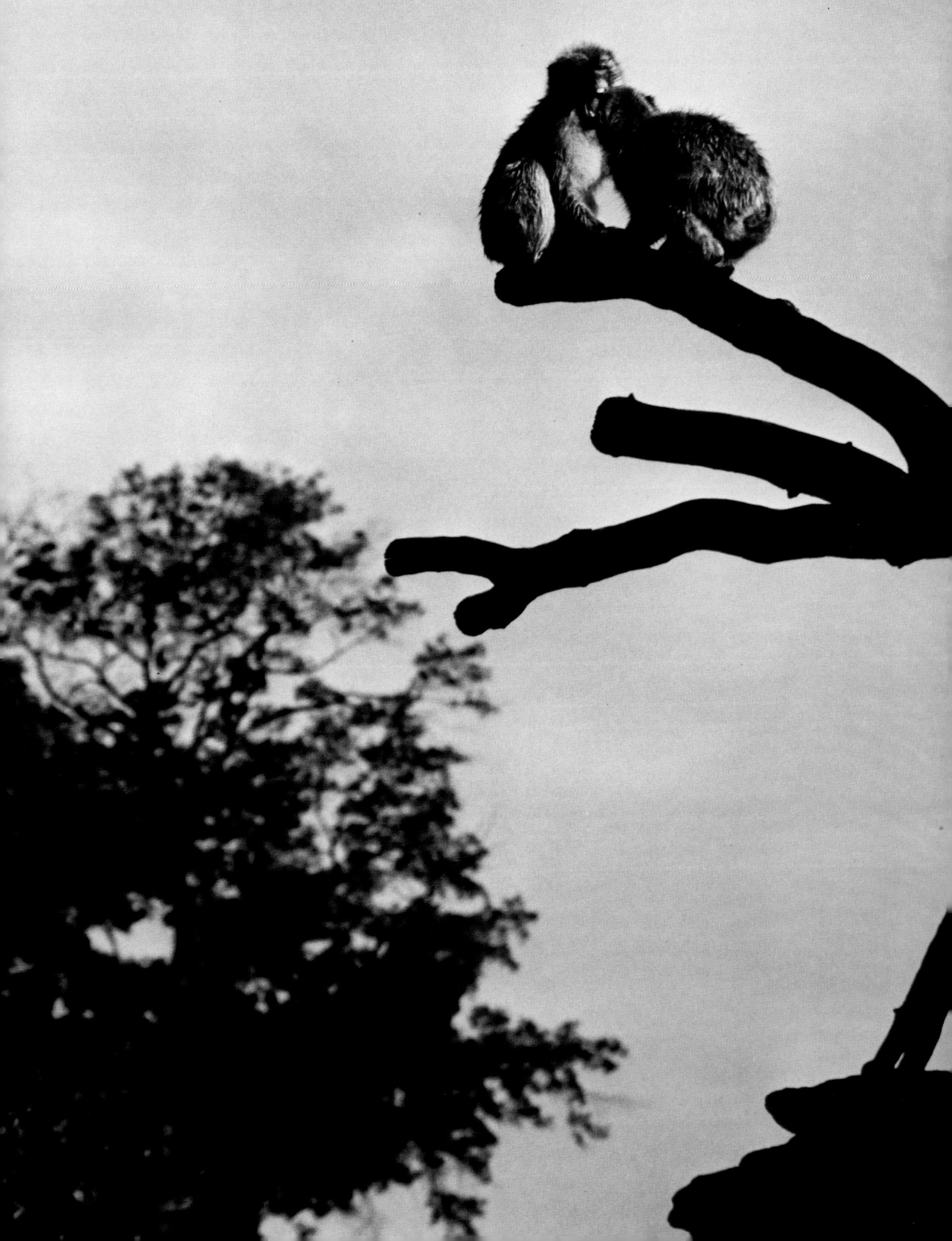

Bactrain Camels

Giraffe

Kings Dominion

White Rhinoceros

Timber Wolf

Timber Wolf

Gray Seal

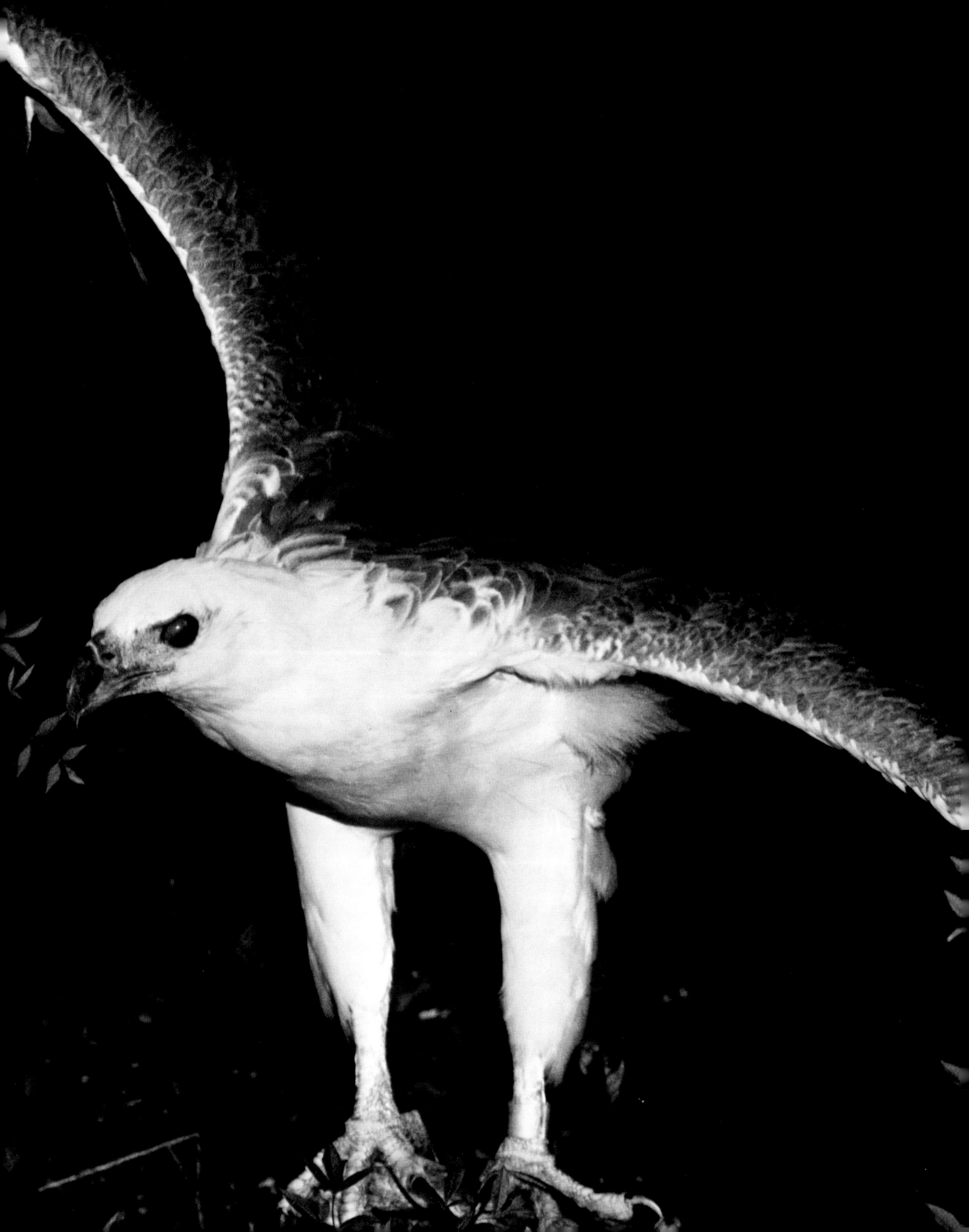

Snowy Owl

ontinued from page 86

Timber Wolf

Timber Wolf

Timber Wolf

Binturong

BINTURONG *(Arctictis binturong)*: The binturong weighs from 20 to 30 pounds. It has long, coarse fur which is a lustrous black color, often with hints of gray, tawny or buff tips. The head is finely specked with gray or buff. The edges of the ears and whiskers are white. The hair on the tail is longer than that on the body. The tail, almost as long as the body, is muscular with a prehensile tip. When resting, the binturong usually lies with the tail covering its head. When moving around, it may utter a series of low grunts or a hissing sound, it growls ferociously when irritated. Despite this seeming wildness, the binturong has been domesticated. It becomes affectionate and follows its master like a dog.

Breeding habits and gestation period are unknown. Females have four mammae.

Their natural diet consists of fruits and other plant matter. Carrion is also included in the diet.

The binturong lives in Burma, Indochina, Thailand, the Malay States, Sumatra, Borneo, and Palawan. It may also live in some of the Indian states. It lives in dense forests where it is considered aboreal and nocturnal.

Raccoon (Backyard)

RACCOON *(Procyon lotor)*: Raccoons vary in weight from 3.3 to 48 pounds. The coloration is gray to almost black. The tail has from five to ten rings and a black streak across the face. They are more nocturnal than diurnal. In the southern parts of the United States, they are active year-round, but in northern climates they hibernate in winter after fattening in the fall. They are not gregarious. The life span is at least 10 years.

Raccoons mate from January to June. They have from one to seven young; usually three to four. In the wild, the young travel with their mother at 10 weeks of age and can go it alone in about one year.

Raccoons are omnivorous, but they prefer frogs, fish, small mammals and birds. They also eat nuts, seeds, fruit, corn and acorns.

The range is southern Canada, throughout most of the United States and Central America. Their habitat is usually wooded and brushy areas near water.

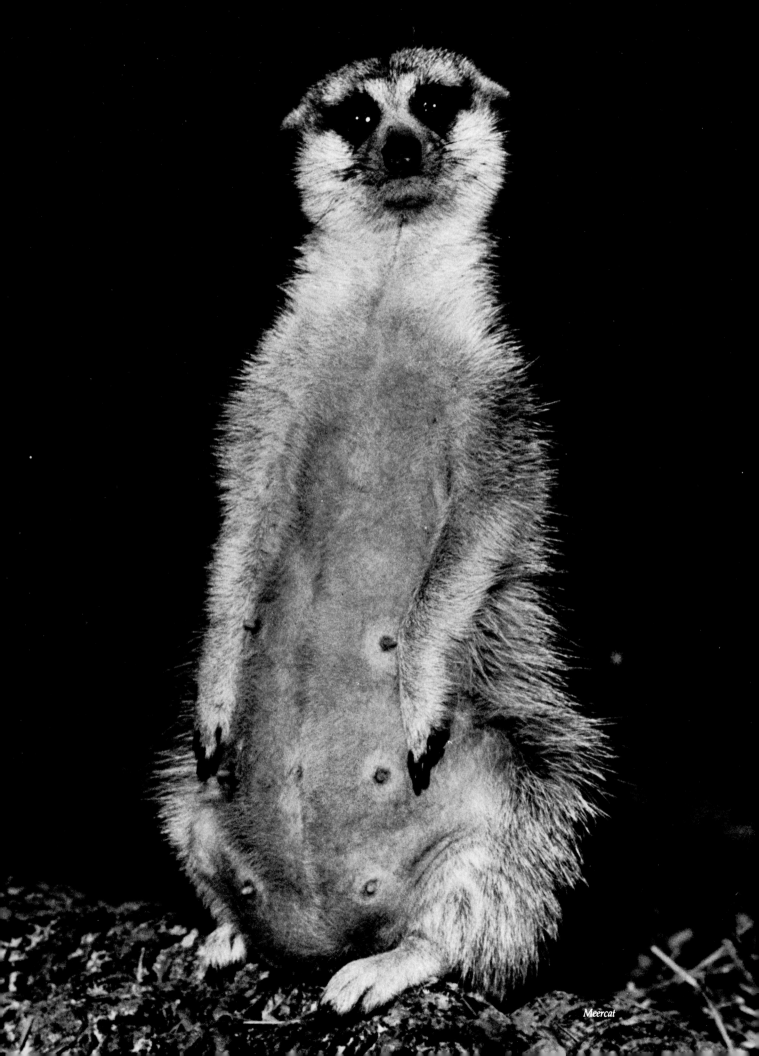

Meercat

MEERCAT (MEERKAT) *(Suricata suricata)*: The coloration of the meercat is light gray; the head is almost white, the ears are black and the tail is yellowish with a black tip. The fur is long and soft with a reddish-brown undercoat. They live in colonies of 25 or more, most of which are thought to be related. They enjoy basking in the sun or characteristically sitting on their haunches surveying the landscape for possible danger. Like prairie dogs, they stay close to their burrows. They often share their burrow systems with the yellow mongoose and the ground squirrel. Meercats tame readily and are affectionate with their masters. Like the domestic cat, they are often kept in homes to kill rats and mice. They have a large variety of sounds, including chatters, whines and alarm barks.

Meercats have been observed to be pregnant in November and February. They have two to five young.

The natural diet of the meercat consists of roots, bulbs, insects (termites and locusts), small mammals, reptiles, birds and eggs.

The meercat ranges throughout South Africa, southwest Africa and Botswana. Their habitat is desert and savannah where they live among rocks and self-dug burrows.

Meercats

144

Hyraxes

ROCK HYRAX *(Heterohyrax syricus)*: The rock hyrax weighs anywhere from one to 10 pounds. Their coloration is brown and whitish, mixed with black. The underside is white. Their hair is thick, short and coarse. They have the appearance of a large guinea pig. They live in colonies containing hundreds of individuals. They like to play among the rocks. The animals are wary, keen of sight and hearing, and will attack anything that disturbs them. They seek shelter at any sign of danger but are very curious and soon show themselves. They are principally diurnal. The chief enemies of hyraxes are pythons. They are also prey to leopards, mongooses and other small carnivores, as well as birds of prey. Their life span is about seven years.

Hyraxes do not seem to have any definite breeding season, although most of the young are born in the latter half of March. They usually have three young after a gestation period of 225 days. The young are able to run about with the others only a few hours after birth.

The natural diet of the hyrax consists of roots, bulbs, and especially locusts. They feed early in the morning, in the late afternoon and in the evening.

Hyraxes live in Ethiopia, Congo, southward through Zimbabwe and southeast Africa. Their habitat consists of rocky mountainous areas, but they range from sea level to an elevation of 2.3 miles.

Tapir

TAPIR *(Tapirus indicus)*: The tapir weighs from 500 to 660 pounds. The Asian tapirs have a coloration that distinguishes them from those of Central and South America. The latter tapirs are dark brown to reddish above, and a paler color below. Tapirs travel alone or in pairs. They are good swimmers and divers. They are generally docile. If threatened, they run into the underbrush or into water. If cornered, they will fight by biting. The chief predators of American tapirs are the jaguar and bears. Tapirs tame easily and quickly adjust to living in captivity. They have been victims of hunting, both for food and sport. The life span is about 30 years.

Breeding among tapirs can take place at any time. The gestation period is 390 to 400 days. The number of young is usually one; rarely two.

Tapirs feed on aquatic vegetation including leaves, buds, and fruit of low-growing plants. They prefer the green shoots of these plants. They have, on occasion, damaged young corn and other grains in Mexico and Central America.

South American tapirs range from Columbia and Venezuela south toward Brazil and Paraguay. In Central America, they range from southern Mexico to South America. Their habitat consists of wooded or grassy areas near a permanent water supply. They live in forests and thickets by day, and forage in grassy or shrubby areas by night.

Gorilla

Gorilla

GORILLA (*Gorilla gorilla*): Gorillas weigh from 300 to 600 pounds in the wild, but go as high as 640 pounds in captivity. Gorillas are the largest and most powerful of the primates. Males are larger than females. Their height is from 4 to 5.7 feet, although their total length is slightly greater than this because their knees are slightly bent. Their hair is coarse and black, becoming silvery gray on the back of all males. Generally, gorillas are quiet and do not molest man unless attacked, annoyed or at bay—at which time they become extremely dangerous. Gorillas live in groups of five to 15, but up to 40 have been observed. The group usually consists of a dominant male, several less dominant males, and many females with their young. The dominant male retains his position only as long as he can defeat the younger males. He is eventually defeated and driven out to thereafter lead a solitary life. The life span of the gorilla has been recorded as 47 years in captivity and 50 years is regarded as the life span in the wild.

The female gorilla bears a single young after a gestation period of about nine months. A baby gorilla born in the National Zoological Park weighed about 4.5 pounds at birth. Females start to menstruate at about eight years of age.

Gorillas are vegetarians. Their diet consists of juicy plants, leaves, berries, ferns and wild banana stems. They climb trees up to 50 feet for food, when necessary.

The lowland gorilla lives in the Ziare river basin (formerly Congo River) from Gabon to the Viringo mountains of Ziare and Uganda. Gorillas have been seen on the coast, although usually some miles from it, and in rain forests at altitudes of up to 10,000 feet. Males spend the night in a shelter at the base of a tree while females spend the night in nests in a tree up to 60 feet above the ground. Nests are built at dusk and occupied only once. Nests are also located in tall grass, undergrowth and overhanging rocks.

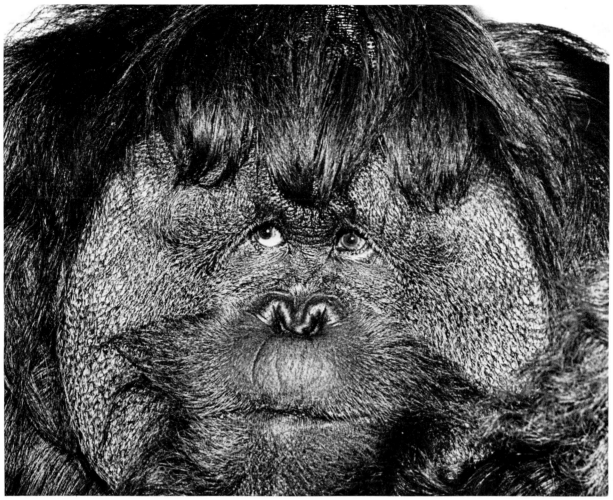

Orangutan

ORANGUTAN *(Pongo pygmaeus)*: Of the primates, orangutans are second in size only to the gorilla. The average weight of the female is 88 pounds and that of the male 165 pounds, although some reach 220 pounds. The coat is thin and shaggy with a reddish-brown coloration. Adult males have cheek pads consisting of subcutaneous fat. The legs are short and relatively weak but the arms, which reach to the ankles when standing, are strong and powerful. Orangutans travel singly, in pairs, or in small family groups. They are diurnal. They are peaceable, gentle and curious toward man when unmolested, but can become extremely dangerous when provoked. Their life span in the wild may be 30 to 40 years.

Orangutans usually have one young. The gestation period is eight to nine months. The newborn is nursed for some time: one in captivity was nursed for six years. Full growth takes from 10 to 12 years, although they are sexually mature at an earlier age.

The natural diet consists of mainly fruit. They also eat leaves, seeds, bark, eggs, young birds and occasionally shellfish.

The orangutan is found only on the islands of Sumatra and Borneo. They live in forests and lowland swamps. Unfortunately, they are now endangered due to the destruction of their natural habitat and hunting.

Barbary Ape

BARBARY APE *(Macaca sylvanus)*: Large Barbary apes weigh up to 29 pounds. Their coloration is yellowish-brown on the back and sides, with lighter color underneath. They live in groups numbering up to 24 comprised of both sexes and all ages. They are strong, fierce fighters when they need be. They are reportedly able to kill a dog in a fair fight. They are agile, both in trees and on the ground. They also swim well. The life span is about 30 years in captivity.

The gestation period is from five to seven months. Usually they have one young, but twins are born occasionally.

The natural diet of the Barbary ape consists of fruits, roots, seeds, insects and grubs.

Barbary apes are found in Gibralter, Morocco and Algeria. They are the only monkeys living wild in Europe. There is a superstition that British rule in Gibralter will end when the last ape leaves the Rock. Their habitat consists of forests, treeless cliffs, rocky areas, and mangrove swamps.

Marmoset

GOLDEN OR LION-HEADED MARMOSET *(Leontideus rosalia)*: The golden marmoset weighs about one-half to a little over 1 pound. The coat is long and silky, and the common name of lion-headed comes from the mane on the head and shoulders which resembles that of the lion. The coloration is a beautiful golden or yellow throughout. They live in family groups consisting of a mated pair and their young, which can number up to eight. They utter high-pitched squeaks. They travel in trees by jumping from branch to branch. Their life span is 15 years in captivity.

The young number from one to two after a gestation period of 132 to 134 days. The father assists in the care of the young. The young ride on the backs of both the father and the mother. The father also gives the young pieces of food when they are old enough to take it. He retains a caring feeling for the young even after they are fully grown. The young are full grown in about one year.

The three known species of marmoset live in trees in the tropical rain forests of eastern Brazil. They are an endangered species.

151

Squirrel Monkey

SQUIRREL MONKEYS *(Saimiri orstedii or sciureus)*: Squirrel monkeys weigh from 1.6 to 2.4 pounds. The coat is short and soft. The usual coloration is white around the eyes, ears, throat and sides of the neck. The top of the head is black to grayish. The back, forearms, hands and feet are reddish or yellow. The shoulders and hind feet are sprinkled with gray. The underparts are whitish or slightly yellow. Males, females, young and old are all colored similarly. They are diurnal and are usually the most plentiful monkeys in a given area. They live together in bands of 12 to 100. Except for faint cries, they are silent. However, they have a louder call when alarmed. Individuals have lived up to nine years in captivity, but in the wild, their life span may be 15 to 20 years.

This monkey has a long breeding season.

Their natural diet consists of insects, spiders, bird eggs, young birds, fruit and nuts.

S. orstedii inhabits Costa Rica and Panama. S. sciureus ranges from northern South America south to Peru, Bolivia, Paraguay and Brazil. S. orstedii frequents scrubby forests, while S. sciureus frequents virgin and secondary forests and cultivated areas, usually along rivers and streams.

Galago

GALAGO *(Galago [4 species])*: The galago is gregarious, arboreal and mostly nocturnal. They have a high-pitched chirping call. Their life span is probably about 10 years.

They usually have one or two young, occasionally three. They are born from April to November after a gestation period of 110 to 120 days.

The natural diet consists of grasshoppers, small birds, eggs, fruits, seeds and flowers.

Their range is Africa, south of the the Sahara, and nearby islands, including Zanzibar. Their habitat is forested and bush regions.

Zebra (Kings Dominion)

ZEBRA *(Equus burchelli bohmi)*: The zebra weighs up to 770 pounds. The coloration is the well-kown dark bands over parts or all of their bodies. They have upright manes of stiff hairs. Zebras are gregarious animals that live in herds of 10 to 12, or mingle in herds of other animals, such as wildebeests or even ostriches. Seasonal gatherings of zebras may number in the hundreds. They are very inquisitive. They can run at speeds up to 40 miles an hour. Zebras are resistant to most African diseases that kill horses. But, efforts to domesticate zebras have been unsuccessful because they are extremely resistant to taming. Zebras are a favorite food of lions, who are their chief enemy. The life span of the zebra is up to 28 years.

The gestation period is 345 to 390 days. One young is born in the spring.

Zebras eat grasses at night and must live near a dependable source of water.

Zebras live in eastern, central and southern Africa. Their habitats consist of plains, savannahs and sometimes mountainous regions.

Wildebeests

WILDEBEEST

(Connochaetes taurinus): The adult, male, white-bearded wildebeest weighs from 500 to 600 pounds. Their coloration is grayish-silver with brownish bands on the neck and shoulders and down to the middle of the body. The face, mane and tail are black and the beard is white. Both the male and female possess horns which rise separately. The horns are heavy and recurved. Wildebeests congregate in herds of five to 15 animals, led by a single bull. Occasionally, they gather in herds of 100

Wildebeests

or more with several bulls. The life span is about 16 years. These animals are also known as gnus, which led to the saying that "no gnus is good news."

Mating of wildebeests occurs in June, and usually one young is born after a gestation period of eight or nine months. The young nurse for eight months but eat grass when only one week old. Cows mate before they are two years old.

Wildebeests forage during the mornings and evenings on karrov bushes and grasses. During the hot part of the day, they relax in available shade.

The range of wildebeests in Africa is from Kenya and Tanzania and southward. Their habitat is open grasslands with nearby water supply.

155

Giraffes

GIRAFFE *(Giraffa camelopardalis)*: The male giraffe weighs up to 3,960 pounds and the female weighs up to 1,200 pounds. Giraffes may reach 11½ feet at the shoulder. Their ground color is buff with dark-reddish to chestnut-brown spots and blotches of various sizes. The underside is light colored and free of spots. Both sexes have two to four short, blunt, horn-like protuberances on the top of the head. Their senses of smell and hearing are very acute. They have the keenest eyesight of any African animals. This, together with their height, gives them the largest range of vision of any land animal. Giraffes can utter low moans or bleats. They are shy, timid and quiet but, because they are gregarious, they usually live in herds of 12 to 15 and sometimes as many as 70 individuals. They can run about as fast as a horse for short distances. Their maximum speed is 29 miles an hour. They can lope along for great distances without tiring. They kick with their front feet if forced to fight and often use their heads to deliver blows, particularly when fighting with another giraffe. Usually they sleep standing up but sometimes they lie down to sleep. Giraffes are preyed upon by lions, and are particularly vulnerable when lying down. Their life span is 15 to 20 years, although one lived 28 years in captivity.

Mating takes place from July to September. One young, rarely two, is born after a gestation period of 420 to 450 days. The young are able to stand about 20 minutes after birth and can nurse withing one hour of birth. They continue to nurse for about nine months. They reach sexual maturity in three to four years.

The natural diet consists of leaves from acacia, mimosa and wild apricot trees. If water is available, they will drink occasionally, consuming up to two gallons a week. However, if water is not available they can go for many weeks, or even months without it.

The range of the giraffe is most of Africa south of the Sahara. They prefer dry savannahs.

156

Dorcas Gazelles

DORCAS GA-ZELLE *(Gazella dorcas)*: Members of the genus Gazella range in weight from 30 to 150 pounds. The coloration varies on the back and sides from brown through fawn and gray to white. Both sexes have horns, except the species 'subgutturosa' where the horns occur only in the males. Gazelles travel singly, in family groups and in herds numbering in the hundreds. The life span is about 10 to 12 years.

Dorcas Gazelles

The young, usually one, are born for the most part in April to June. A few days after birth, they are able to follow their mothers and within a week, they can run almost as fast as their parents.

Gazelles feed on succulent desert plants, acacia trees, locusts and locust larvae.

Members of this genus range from northern and eastern Africa to Arabia, Israel, Syria; central Asia from Turkey to Mongolia; and into the plains of India. They live on plains and on rocky, sandy desert lands.

Bactrian Camels

BACTRIAN CAMEL *(Camelus bactrianus)*: There are two species of camel; the dromedary is one-humped and the bactrian is two-humped. The bactrian camel stands up to 6.9 feet at the shoulder and weighs up to 1,500 pounds. The coloration varies from deep brown to dusty gray. They have long hairs on the head, neck, humps, thighs and tip of the tail. The rest of the body is covered with a shaggy wool. When camels shed their winter coats, the wool comes off in big chunks giving the animal a ragged, rough appearance. The camel is noted for its ability to go for long periods without water. Although adapted to conservation of water, they actually cannot store reserve water in the body. If forced to go a long time without water, they do so at the risk of losing both weight and strength. When the camel is well-fed, the hump is erect and plump but when they do not have enough food, the hump shrinks and may lean to one side. In the wild, the bactrian camel lives alone and in pairs, but generally in groups of four to six. Groups of 12 to 15 are rare. Camels are able to withstand extremes of heat and cold. They are good swimmers. They will drink brackish or even salt water if necessary. Camels restore body water by drinking up to 14 gallons of water. In the middle of the 19th century, camels were introduced to the southwestern United States for transportation puposes. It was even though that they could supplant beef cattle. However, the advent of the railroad and other conditions prevented this experiment from success. The camel's life span is from 17 to 50 years.

One (rarely two) calf is born after a gestation period of 370 to 440 days. The newborn calf has soft fleece, utters a gentle "bah," and can move about freely within 24 hours. The young becomes independent in four years and reaches full growth in five years. Females breed every other year and can produce 12 calves in a lifetime.

The natural diet consists of any vegetation that grows in the desert or semi-desert areas. If forced by extreme hunger, they will eat fish, meat, bones and skin. They can eat salty plants that are rejected by most animals.

The range of the dromedary camel is uncertain because this species is fully domesticated, but it was probably in the region now known as Arabia. The range of the bactrian camel is China, Turkestan and Mongolia. Their habitat is the Gobi steppes along the rivers but when the snows arrive, they move into the dessert.

Two-Toed Sloth

TWO-TOED SLOTH *(Choloepus didactylus)*: The two-toed sloth weighs up to 20 pounds. Its coat consists of long guard hairs with a short undercoat. The coloration is grayish-brown with a light colored face. The arms and legs are long. They have two fingers bound together with skin the entire length, and each finger has a large hook-like claw. The hind feet have three toes with hook-like claws. Sloths spend almost their entire lives in an upside-down position; eating, sleeping, mating and even giving birth in that position. They do, however, swim with the body upright. Almost all of their movements are extremely slow. They defend themselves by striking quickly with their long arms and large hooked claws. They also use their teeth for biting. Sloths have the lowest variable body temperature of any mammal. Their temperature ranges from a low of 24 degrees Celsius to a high of 33 degrees Celsius. Sloths have survived due to several factors—namely, camouflage (they look like a bunch of dried leaves when sleeping), remaining motionless during the day, nocturnal activities, heavy fur and thick skin, and an extremely strong will to live. Their life span in captivity is at least 11 years.

A single youngster is produced after a gestation period of at least 263 days. The young eat solid food within one month. The offspring hooks its claws on the mother's breast and abdomen where it remains while she climbs or rests.

Their natural diet consists of leaves, tender twigs and fruit.

The range of the sloth is Venezuela, the Guianas and northern Brazil. They live in forested areas.

Gray Seal

GRAY SEAL *(Halichoerus grypus)*: Male gray seals weigh up to 640 pound and females up to 550 pounds. The coloration is light or dark gray, sometimes almost black on the upper parts, usually with spots or blotches. The underside is a lighter color. The young are white and wooly. Gray seals are gregarious. They can dive to at least 420 feet. In the East Atlantic and Baltic Sea, most of the young disperse from the home colony and spend their first two years at sea. However, some of the young remain near the breeding areas. Gray seals feed alone and rest in small groups on land. They go to traditional sites to breed. The world's population is estimated at 25,000 to 50,000. The life span is up to 18 years.

Breeding groups consist of one bull and up to 10 cows. The young pups are born on the ice in late winter or late spring in the west Atlantic. In the east Atlantic, the young are born on the shore in the fall. The number of young is usually one; rarely two. The pups nurse for two weeks. Cows usually breed again within two weeks after the birth of the pups.

The natural diet of the gray seal is fish and cuttlefish.

Gray seals live in the temperate waters of the north Atlantic, and a few live southward to the Channel Islands of France. They favor turbulent waters near cliffs, rocks and reefs. They also like estuaries, as well as sand and pebble beaches.

Egyptian Spiny Mouse

EGYPTIAN SPINY MOUSE *(Acomys cahirinus)*: The adult Egyptian spiny mouse weighs from about 1.8 to 3.7 ounces. The coloration on the back is pale yellowish or reddish-brown, reddish or dark gray—it's belly is white. The body and tail are covered with coarse, stiff spines. The tail is brittle and easily broken. This is why they are also called porcupine mice.

The young, numbering from one to five, are usually born between February and September. Gestation is about 42 days. The weight of the newborn is 0.2 ounces. Spiny mice live communally in groups. The female will often help other females give birth. She may nurse another female's young or even adopt them.

Spiny mice are omnivorous, but their food consists mainly of plant material and grain.

Several species of spiny mice range from Pakistan through southern Iran and into Israel, Arabia and most of Africa. Their usual habitat is rocky areas, although one species inhabits sandy valleys. They also live in crevices of termite dwellings with dense vegetation. The Egyptian species lives mainly near human habitat; hence their name.

Short-Tailed, Leaf-Nosed Bat

Short-Tailed, Leaf-Nosed Bat

BAT, SHORT-TAILED, LEAF-NOSED *(Carollia perspicillata)*: The length of
the head and body is 48 to 65 mm, the tail ranges from 3 to 14 mm, and the
forearm is 34 to 45 mm. The weight is 0.35 to 0.75 ounces. The coloration is
dark brown to rusty. Bats roost upside down singly, in small groups, and in
colonies of hundreds to thousands. They are swift fliers who use sonar for
guidance.

These bats have more than one breeding season in the Amazon region, and
in Panama they breed throughout the year. Mature females have twins, but
younger females have single offspring. Males and females live together.

The natural diet consists of fruits such as guavas, bananas, wild figs, and
plantains. They also eat nectar and small insects. They are guided to ripened
fruit by their acute sense of smell. They begin feeding at dusk. In some tropical
areas, fruits have to be harvested green because of the bats.

This species of bats live in Mexico and southward to Peru and southern
Brazil. They live in caves, tunnels, culverts, abandoned buildings and hollow
trees.

Bald Eagle

CHAPTER VII

Birds

The distinguishing characteristic of birds is their feathers. A creature with feathers is a bird; one without feathers is not a bird. Flight, however, is not a universal attribute of birds. There are a number of flightless birds, such as kiwis, ostriches, rheas, emus, and cassowaries. These birds protect themselves by speed, strength and cunning. Likewise, birds are not the only creatures that can fly albeit, except for the bat, they are not nearly as accomplished in flight as the birds. Some power of flight has been developed by flying fish, East Indian flying lizards, and mammals, including bats, some marsupials, the flying squirrel and some monkeys. Man has envied the power of flight in birds since antiquity. Man has finally achieved this power with the aid of flying machines and rockets.

Unlike the reptiles to whom they are related, but like mammals, birds are warm-blooded. That is, they maintain a constant body temperature that averages about 10 F degrees above that of the mammals, including man. This enables birds to withstand colder climates than cold-blooded creatures can. It is interesting in this connection, that although cold-blooded, the closest relatives of birds and, in fact, their ancestors are the reptiles, who are cold-blooded. The skeletal structure of the bird is similar to that of reptiles. Birds still retain the scaled feet of the reptile.

According to O. L. Austin in his book, "Birds of the World," the number of species of extant and recently extinct birds is 8,650. Ornithologists are still discovering new species at a rate of one or two a year. However, it is doubtful if more than 100 species remain to be discovered because there are not many unexplored places left in the world.

Man has been directly or indirectly responsible for the extinction of many species of birds. Man's harmful activities include destruction of habitats, hunting for food and sport, and poisoning the food chain with massive use of insecticides, such as DDT. Present day destruction of habitat is proceeding at an alarming rate in the South American rain forests. It also proceeds almost everywhere in the world as populations explode with devastating effects. There is a growing awareness of man's destructive activities and a growing concern, and even actions, to prevent this modern, natural holocaust.

The length of birds as used in this chapter is measured from the tip of the bill to the tip of the tail with the bird laid flat on its back and the neck normally extended, as mentioned by Austin.

Bald Eagle

BALD EAGLE *(Haliaeetus leucoephalus)*: The bald eagle is 34 inches long. The bald eagle belongs to the Accipetriadae family, the largest family of raptors (birds which prey on other creatures with bill and claw). There are 70 genera and 205 species of highly varied forms in this family. They range in size from the sharp-shinned hawk, only slightly larger than the quail, to the great sloth-killing harpy eagle of the Amazon jungle. The bald eagle acquires its characteristic white tail and head only upon reaching maturity at four to five years of age. Up to that time, the bald eagle is a uniform, flecked brownish color. The bald eagle was adopted as the central figure in the Great Seal of the United States by the Continental Congress in 1782. The number of bald eagles declined alarmingly in the 1950s and 1960s, primarily due to the heavy use of the insecticide DDT. DDT in the food chain of the eagles caused thinning of the egg shells which resulted in excessive breakage. Also, the insecticide caused failure to hatch in those eggs that did not break. In 1972, DDT was banned as an insecticide and the decline in the bald eagle was reversed, but it is still struggling to rebuild its population.

Bald Eagle

The bald eagle builds a bulky nest of twigs and small branches in a treetop. They mate for life and return to the same spot year after year. Destruction of the nests and nesting trees has made their come back more difficult. They lay only two eggs at a time.

The bald eagle catches waterfowl and marsh rabbits and will kill larger animals when it can, including spotted fawns. The greater part of their diet consists of live fish and those found dead along the shore. Bald eagles have a habit of harassing Ospreys causing them to drop fish that they have caught. The eagle then retrieves them, often catching them in the air.

The bald eagle ranges throughout North America. It has become rare in most of the lower United States but is still plentiful in Alaska.

Bald Eagle

Bald Eagle

White-Bellied Sea Eagle

WHITE-BELLIED SEA EAGLE *(Haliaeetus leucogaster)*: This bird is from 27 to 31 inches in length. It is nearly as large as the bald eagle. It is slate gray and white in color. The white is on the under side. It is usually seen singly or in pairs perched on tall trees or soaring over water and coastal areas.

Sea Eagle

This sea eagle builds a large platform nest of sticks either in a tree top or on a rocky crag, but always near water. The nest is sparsely lined with green leaves. Two, rarely three, white eggs are laid in the nest, incubated principally by the female with occasional assistance by the male.

The natural diet is principally fish, but they also eat sea snakes, river snakes, small crocodiles and river carrion. The sea eagle particularly likes sea snakes. It catches the snake as it rises to the surface for air, snatching it into the air, and killing it by clamping its talons onto its head. Like other eagles and the osprey, the sea eagle causes whistling kites to drop their prey and catches it before it hits the water.

The range of the sea eagle is from India and Sri Lanka, eastward through the Malayan Archipelago to Tasmania, Australia and New Guinea. Its habitat is the sea, the sea coast, and the larger inland waterways and rivers. Sometimes it flys over savannahs long distances from water.

Sea Eagle

Sea Eagle

Imperial Eagle

Imperial Eagle

IMPERIAL EAGLE *(Aquila heliaca)*: There are two species of imperial eagles—the Spanish imperial eagle has a white crown and is either extinct or nearly so; the eastern species seems to be holding its own in the Mediterranean area.

Imperial Eagle

Snowy Owl

Snowy Owl

SNOWY OWL *(Nyctea scandiaca)*: The snowy owl is 25 inches long. The owl, like the domestic cat, has had a sinister reputation of association with the occult, sorcery, evil spirits, witches and demons. This reputation has been enhanced by the eerie cries of some of these owls in the night. And, as with the cat, this reputation is unfounded. Snowy owls are diurnal hunters, unlike most of the owls. They have extremely large eyes; larger than they appear to be. The eyeball of the snowy owl is almost as large as that of a man. This gives them a tremendously acute vision. They also have a very well developed sense of hearing. They can fly fast enough to catch a duck in flight.

Snowy owls breed circumpolarly in the tundra areas. They nest in the open on the ground, usually on a slight elevation so that they can watch for approaching enemies. Snowy owls' reproduction is tied to the abundance of food, which is cyclic. When food, in the form of rabbits and lemmings, is plentiful, snowy owls lay from seven to 10 white, almost spherical eggs. But, when the food supply wanes, they lay only two to three eggs and in very lean times, they do not nest at all.

Owls eat any animal that they can kill. Their main diet consists of lemmings and arctic hares. When a food scarcity occurs every five to seven years, they are forced south in their search for food. They show up as far south as the British Isles, northern Germany, the Soviet Union, southern Siberia, northern Japan, and eastern and central United States.

Normally snowy owls live in arctic regions and remain there except when food shortages occur.

Snowy Owl

Brown Wood Owl

BROWN WOOD OWL *(Genus, Strix)*: The natural diet of this owl has great variety; including lizards, other reptiles, amphibians, birds, squirrels and small rodents. Owls swallow their prey whole and then digest with strong digestive juices. The undigestible material, including bones, fur and feathers are formed into pellets which the owl ejects by coughing up. Contents of these pellets give clues to the extensive diet range. Owls usually come back to a favorite perch to eat their prey. Consequently, sometimes hundreds of these pellets are found on the ground under this perch. The presence of a northern Red-backed Pine Mouse (Pitmys) was unsuspected in central Connecticut until the skulls of several were discovered in pellets dropped by a Barn owl.

These owls live in southeast Asia and India.

Brown Wood Owl

Brown Wood Owl

Tawny Frogmouth Owl

TAWNY FROGMOUTH OWL *(Podargus strigoides)*: The tawny frogmouth owl is 19 inches long. These owls have soft, silky plumage with an intricate pattern of streaks and barrings. The overall coloration is graying to brownish. The sexes are alike. They are nocturnal, and during the day they sleep lengthwise on a branch that blends well into the surroundings. Their legs are short and their feet small. The call of the frogmouth during the night is a distinctive "oom-oom." They have large, flat, horny triangular hooked bills. In hunting, they catch their prey on the ground instead of on the wing, as most owls do.

Frogmouth owls nest in trees usually, in the fork of a horizontal branch. In some cases they build nests with twigs and at other times use their own feathers. Females lay one or two eggs. Both sexes incubate the eggs—the female takes the night shift and the male takes the day shift. The young are covered with down and remain in the nest until they can fly.

The natural diet of this owl consists mainly of insects such as beetles, centipedes, scorpions, caterpillars, and sometimes even live mice.

The frogmouth owl ranges from Australia northward to Tasmania, Malaya and the Philippines, and eastward to the Solomon Islands.

Tawny Frogmouth Owl

Andean Condor

**ANDEAN CON-
DOR** *(Vultur gryphus)*:
The condor family
contains two of the
largest living flying
birds. The Andean con-
dor is 52 inches in
length. It weighs from
20 to 25 pounds and
has a wing span of 10
feet. They are strong
winged and great fliers
with great soaring abil-
ity. The Andean condor
is rare but is not in
danger of extinction as
is the California con-
dor. The life span is not
known, but they have
lived up to 50 years in
zoos.

Andean Condor

The diet of the con-
dor is carrion and animal refuse. They seldom attack live prey, but sometimes
kill helpless young animals. Their beaks are too weak to tear freshly killed flesh
and they must wait until it is partly rotted before they can eat it.

Andean condors lay comparatively small clutches of eggs and the incubation period is long. They rear their young in the nest.

The Andean condor ranges from Venezuela and Columbia to Patagonia in
the south. It lives in the high Andes mountains where it covers a wide range of
sparsely settled territory. Consequently, its chances for survival are better than
that of the California condor.

Andean Condor

Andean Condor

Andean Condor

King Vulture

KING VULTURE *(Sarcoramphus papa)*: The king vulture is 32 inches in length. It is the third largest of the American vultures following the Andean and California condors in size. The body is basically black and white. The head is naked and brilliantly colored in purple, green and yellow. They do not attain these colors until they acquire adult plumage at three to four years of age. It has a wart covered head. Vultures are great soaring birds but lack the physical strength and equipment of the other raptors like eagles, falcons and owls. Their beaks are too weak to tear flesh until it has partly rotted. American vultures are voiceless and can only make weak hissing sounds. Vultures are noted for their keen eyesight. They soar from tree top level to heights of hundreds of feet on thermal updrafts. They are not gregarious but they often roost together and tend to gather in large numbers when food is available.

The natural diet of the king vulture, like that of its cousins, consists mainly of carrion, although they sometimes kill helpless young mammals.

The king vulture ranges from the rain forests of southern Mexico southward to Argentina.

Rhea

RHEA (*Rhea americana*): The rhea is commonly known as the South American ostrich, although they are considerably smaller than ostriches. The rhea stands four to five feet tall and weighs up to 50 pounds. Ostriches, on the other hand, stand eight feet tall and weigh up to 300 pounds. The rhea is the largest bird in America. Rheas travel in small flocks, often with a herd of deer for protection. They depend on their speed to escape their enemies. Like the ostrich, their wings are useless for flight. The wings are longer, but they

Rhea

lack tail plumage and their body plumage is softer than that of the ostrich. Rheas are swift runners. From a standing start, they can outrun the fastest horse. These birds tend to hide in tall grass and double back on their tracks which makes them easy prey. Rheas roamed the pampas in large numbers but they have been decimated by loss of habitat and hunting for sport, food and feathers. The male has a loud booming voice which carries great distances but the females have no voice. They tame easily and make good pets.

Rhea males are polygamous with a harem of five or six hens. The males do most of the work in rearing the young. They prepare huge nests, at least three feet in diameter, lined with grass. The various hens lay 20 to 30 yellow to greenish eggs in the nest, sometimes up to 50 eggs about five inches long. The male starts to incubate the eggs which takes up to six weeks. If the hens try to lay more eggs after the incubation starts, the male chases them away forcing them to lay them on the ground in the open. The chicks have a high-pitched whistle. The male takes care of the chicks for six weeks at which time they are on their own.

The natural diet of the rhea includes a great variety of vegetables and other plant material, as well as insects and small mammals.

The rhea ranges over the pampas of Brazil and Argentina.

Cassowary

CASSOWARY *(Casuarius bicarunculatus)*: The New Guinea cassowary is 52 inches long. Cassowaries are heavy-bodied with short, strong legs. They cannot fly. Their plumage is coarse and hard which makes a thick mat to protect the birds from the thorny undergrowth of their habitat. Further protection is afforded by a bony helmet on the forehead which wards off potentially harmful obstacles in the rough undergrowth. The color of the skin on the featherless heads and necks contain vivid reds, blues, purples and yellows. Two species have brilliant wattles hanging from their heads. Females are larger than males. Cassowaries are naturally shy and partially nocturnal. They are, however, extremely bad-tempered and have attacked and killed humans who provoked them. They attack by slashing feet-first with their powerful claws. The inner claw has a long, sharp spike making it a particularly vicious, and even lethal weapon. Cassowaries can run at speeds of up to 30 miles an hour even through thick underbrush. They can also swim jungle rivers. Their voices are harsh, hoarse, croaking with various squeaks, howls, grunts, snorts and bellows—definitely not very pleasant.

Cassowaries are thought to be monogamous. Their nest is a shallow structure made of leaves on the forest floor into which the female deposits three to six large, dark green eggs. The male incubates the eggs without help from the female. The young, upon hatching, are striped lengthwise in a very effective camouflage pattern. Both male and female care for the young.

The natural diet is mainly berries, fruit and plant material, insects and even some small animals.

The cassowary is native to Australia, New Guinea and other islands in this area. They dwell in the dense jungle forests in the thick, thorny undergrowth.

186

Black Swan

BLACK SWAN

(Chenopis atrata): The black swan is 56 to 60 inches long. It is a member of the group of waterfowl that includes ducks and geese. Swans are the largest of this group of birds and their necks are longer than their bodies. Despite their size, the swan is extremely graceful. Most of the members of this group are very gregarious. The black swan has curly feathers, bright red bill and white wing feathers that show only when in flight.

Black Swan

The black swan is native to Australia and Tasmania. It has been domesticated and introduced into New Zealand where large flocks exist in semi-wild state.

Black-Necked Swan

BLACK-NECKED SWAN *(Cygnus melancoriphus)*: The black-necked swan is 42 inches long. It breeds on the British-owned Falkland Islands. It is native to southern South America, ranging from southern Brazil through Argentina and Chile south to Patagonia.

188

Saurus Cranes

Saurus Cranes

SARUS CRANE *(Grus antigone)*: The sarus crane is 60 inches in length. Cranes, as a group, are long-legged and long-necked birds. They fly with their necks straight out in front. When migrating, cranes travel up to two miles high in V or long echelon formations. Cranes engage in characteristic dancing ceremonies which is not only part of courtship, but is also just a display of liveliness and good feelings. Cranes tame easily and breed well in captivity. This is fortunate because they are a desperately endangered family. Cranes possess noticeable longevity. The life span is probably between 50 and 100 years.

Cranes build their nests on the ground surrounded by water from local vegetation. Usually two, and rarely three, gray to brown spotted eggs are deposited in the nest. The incubation period varies from 28 to 35 days. Males and females share in nest building, incubation and caring for the chicks. Young can run as soon as they are hatched and, although they grow rapidly, it requires about 10 weeks to learn to fly. Cranes breed only once a year.

The natural diet of cranes varies widely. It includes both vegetable and animal material, although vegetable matter predominates. They eat grass, and tender roots, as well as insects and insect larvae, worms, snails, amphibians, reptiles, fish, small birds and mammals.

The sarus crane ranges across southeast Asis to India and the Philippines. Their habitat consists of marshlands, wet plains, prairies, sandy flatlands and seashores.

WHITE PELICAN

(Pelacanus onocrotalus): The white pelican is 65 inches in length. The pelican's pouch holds almost three gallons which is about three times the capacity of its stomach. Pelicans are very gregarious; they nest in colonies, remain together in flocks away from breeding grounds, nest together, fly together in V or echelon formations, and indulge in cooperative fishing. They fish by forming a crescent on the water some distance from the shore. Then, as though on command, they all move toward the shore with beating wings and feet driving the fish into shallow waters in a closing arc. As the fish are driven to the shallows, the pelicans catch them in flailing beak and pouch.

Pelicans usually nest on the ground and lay the eggs in a hollow lined with sticks and vegetation. Sometimes they build their nests in low trees, bushes, or mangroves. These nests are built on a platform of sticks and reeds. The female pelican lays from one to four white eggs which are incubated alternately by both sexes. Newly hatched chicks are fed by regurgitation of partially digested food into their mouths. This is very difficult for the first week because the chicks cannot hold their heads up. Within a week, the chicks can put their heads into the parent's pouch. Chicks can fly in two months but mature slowly. It requires three years to acquire full plumage, and they probably do not breed for three or four years.

Pelican

The natural diet of the pelican is about four pounds of fish daily. It takes about 150 pounds to rear a chick to the flying stage. Fortunately for the pelican, their diet consists of fish with no commercial value.

The Old World white pelican lives in southern Europe, Africa, southern Asia and southward to Australia. The American white pelican lives from British Columbia and Ontario southward to Texas.

CHAPTER VIII

Reptiles

Many think of snakes as the only members of the Reptilia Class of animals. In addition to snakes, this class contains turtles and tortoises, lizards, worm lizards, tuatora and crocodilians. Of a total of 6,547 species in 48 families of reptiles, snakes comprise 36.5 percent, compared with 57.3 percent for lizards. Turtles and tortoises comprise 3.7 percent, worm lizards 2.1 percent, tuatoras 0.02 percent and crocodilians 0.1 percent.

Reptiles have a large range of sizes. Length ranges from four inches for turtles to 37½ feet for snakes. Weights range up to 1500 pounds for the huge leatherback turtle, which attains a length of six feet.

Reptiles have worldwide distribution. As a class, they are omnivorous. Body temperatures of reptilia are maintained externally, in contrast with birds and mammals whose temperature is regulated internally.

Reproduction in reptiles occurs in three ways: eggs, live-born young and parthenogenesis; that is by self fertilization of female-only species.

Longevity of reptiles varies greatly. It is one to two years for worm lizards, 50 years for lizards, 100 to 200 years for turtles and 120 years (probably) for tuatoras.

The colors of reptiles vary in many ways—from dull and dark to bright, mixed and patterned. Chameleons have the ability to change colors in order to blend with the colors and patterns of their environment. This ability is an aid in capturing food as well as in protection from predators.

WATER DRAGON *(Physignathus cocincinus)*: The water dragon lives in mainland southeast Asia. The habitat is tropical forests and trees alongside streams. Their natural diet consists of invertebrates, small birds and small mammals.

ALDABRA TORTOISE *(Geochelone gigantea)*: The Aldabra giant tortoise is nearly five feet long and weighs up to 250 pounds. The habitat is grassy plains and scrub areas. The natural diet consists of grasses and other plant materials.

GREEN IGUANA *(Iguana iguana)*: The green iguana ranges from Mexico to Central Brazil. Their habitat consists of rain forests and dry forests, in trees and often near water. Their natural diet consists of vegetation, fruits and some insects.

Green Iguana

Aldabra Turtle

CHAPTER IX

Survival

Following is a list of current or recent practices in the treatment of animals. These are more or less randomly selected from among scores of examples.

1. Use of steel, leg-hold traps is one of the worst. These are fiendish devices that sometimes force animals to chew their legs off in order to escape.

2. Killing eagles from a helicopter.

3. Killing coyotes, bears and other animals from the air.

4. Indiscriminate poisoning of predators, particularly the killing of coyotes by a practice called "denning"—that is, killing pups in their dens with poison. (Real sporting, you know.)

5. Killing of rhinoceroses for their horns which are used for dagger handles, aphrodisiacs, quack medicines and other equally trivial things.

6. Killing of elephants for their tusks to be used to make decorative trinkets.

7. Killing helpless baby seals by clubbing them to death.

8. Outlaw killing of sperm whales by the Japanese fishing industry.

9. Killing spotted cats for the fur industry.

10. The fur trade itself is obscene.

11. Slaughter of dolphins by the Japanese fishing industry.

12. Slaughter of dolphins by commercial fishermen.

13. Sports hunting.

14. Stealing of pets for sale to research laboratories.

15. Deliberate running down of stray animals beside the road by some motorists.

16. Maltreatment of animals used for scientific experiments in research laboratories.

17. Indiscriminate use of poisonous insecticides.

18. Human over-population and its resultant destruction of animal habitats.

19. Use of drugs in thoroughbred horse racing that frequently cause the horse to break down during the race.

The foregoing are only some of the assaults on animals by humans. Proponents of these citations will make all sorts of ratioinalizations to excuse their particular form of animal abuse.

Deer

As I contemplate the treatment of animals by some people, my feelings progress from rage and frustration to sorrow that I cannot do more to alleviate the situation. In the throes of these emotions, I have lashed out and admitted that I am ashamed to be a member of the human race. This shame applies to the net results only. Humanity as a whole cannot be condemned for this because there are many good people devoting their lives to stemming this tide of cruelty and destruction before it is too late. These people are making progress, but it is still in the balance as to whether or not it is too late.

One cannot blame prehistoric man for his contribution to the extinction of certain animals (the mammoth, for example). Here we had a more or less equal struggle for survival that required considerable bravery on the part of man. In contrast, Ugandan leader, Idi Amin used advanced military equipment to blast elephants, hippopotamuses and other animals merely to gratify his sadistic mind. Although protests were made at the time, they were not loud enough to be effective before great damage was done. At last report, Amin is living out his life in an Arab country.

We have many small-scaled Idi Amins in our own country and throughout the world. They are called sports hunters. They use modern firearms to gun down animals without qualm. It must bolster their macho egos to do this. One excuse is that they love the outdoors and the beauty of nature. But, the climax of their love is to blast some innocent, wild animal to death in this beautiful, peaceful natural setting. Some love of nature.

Humans, through some mysterious circumstance have risen to a position of life or death power over all other creatures of the earth. With this awesome power should go a responsibility for the welfare of these other creatures. These other animals must be respected for having survived in the savage world, without all of man's advantages, longer than humans .

It is the failure of mankind to recognize and exercise these responsibilities that has led to the flagrant abuses going on all around us. Greed, ignorance and indifference are the root causes of our neglect. These forces are thoroughly intrenched in our world. But, thanks to the efforts of those who have devoted their lives to animal welfare, we are making progress in alleviating the evils of animal cruelty. Education is the best long-term hope of making progress in this area.

It is ironic that man, with all his gifts, has outsmarted himself by inventing atomic weapons. We are all now vulnerable to the destruction of the planet by the insane action of just one world leader. Here again, education is the key to our survival.

The natural beauty of women needs no enhancement by wearing furs of dead animals than does the lily need gilding.

Deer

Hippopotamuses

CHAPTER X

On Zoo Animal Photography

Successful zoo animal photography has several problems inherent in the zoo setting. Principal among these problems are cage bars and wires, bad backgrounds, reflections from glass enclosures (including flare from flash lights), and the intensity and quality of the available indoor lighting. These obstacles must be overcome either in taking the photograph or in the darkroom to have a satisfactory photograph. The photograph should simulate, as nearly as possible, animals in their natural settings.

I used Hasselblad cameras for my photographs in the zoo. The larger negative, compared to the 35 mm format, is an obvious advantage in obtaining sharp pictures.

Cage bars and wires can be removed by getting close enough to put the lens shade through the spaces between them. If this cannot be done, putting the lens shade in contact with the bars so that they will disappear due to selective focus. When flash lighting is used, it is necessary to provide a shield so the light does not shine on the bars or wires directly in front of the lens. It can be reflected into the lens and yet still light the animal subject. This requires some ingenuity on the part of the photographer, and how it is accomplished varies according to the equipment being used. If one is standing farther back, bars and wires can be eliminated by selective focus in some cases. However, flash cannot be used in these cases because reflection from the bars will show up in the photograph.

White Tiger & Cubs (Tiger by the tail)

Sometimes a restraining rail prevents one from getting close to the bars or wires. This is the case with the leopards and jaguars at the National Zoo. I devised a support for my camera and flash light that consisted of a 1 x 2 inch board, about 6 feet long. Two screws were put through the end of this stick so that it could be hooked between the wires of the cage. The camera was set in place on the end of this stick so that the lens was either flush with the bars or nearly so. Thus, you can easily get the camera into position while remaining outside the protective railing. Then, focus the camera from outside the railing and correct the setting by subtracting the distance between the railing and the camera. Hook this support between the bars and point the camera at the subject. I use a camera with electric shutter release and film advance so that taking the photograph is no problem. In the case of the leopards, a spotted one attacked this device but did not damage the camera due to the protection provided by the wires. This device is not too satisfactory, but I was able to get some very good photographs of both the leopards and jaguars.

Removal of bad backgrounds in caged animal photographs also requires some ingenuity. Experimental positioning of the camera will usually do the trick because even in the cages, most animals have natural settings. In black and white photography, much can be done in the dark room to remove obtrusive backgrounds. In outdoor photography, the same principles apply in elimination of distractions in the backgrounds.

Reflections are extremely difficult to cope with in photographing animals behind glass. One of the worst places for reflection is inside the ape house at the National Zoo. If you can get up to the glass, putting the lens shade of the camera in contact with the glass is the best way to eliminate reflections, although even then it is necessary to check for them and alter position if necessary. If you are too far back to contact the glass, the only way to eliminate reflections is to move around until they can no longer be seen in the view finder.

Flare from flash lights is another problem in photographing animals through glass. It is necessary to have the flash "off" the plane of the camera lens. I do this with a device that raises the flash at least 10 inches above the center of the lens, and in my case, about six inches to the left. This not only prevents flare, but also helps in modeling the subject. Ideally, elimination of flare is accomplished by having the flash in the raised position and the lens shade resting against the glass. This also steadies the camera and therefore minimizes camera movement. If you cannot get next to the glass, having the flash in the raised position eliminates flare, even when there is several feet distance. Those with the flash built into the camera cannot eliminate flare from the glass. In addition, the eyes of the animals will probably show up red because of light reflection from the back of the eye. It is surprising that photographing through reasonably clean glass has no deleterious effect on the image.

Use of a tripod certainly eliminates fuzzy photographs due to camera movement, and their use is recommended whenever possible. One serious drawback of using a tripod is the loss of mobility so necessary in animal photography. Thus, many good photgraphs can be lost while positioning the camera on the tripod. I have used a tripod successfully in a few cases where it could be set up in anticipation of the animal being in a certain position. For the most part, I prefer to hand hold my camera using a "handlebar" grip. This gives me the mobility I need to get the pictures I want. Effect of camera movement is minimized by using a fast film and an exposure time of 1/500 second. Use of a fast film also permits use of maximum **f** stop to give maximum depth of field at 1/500 second.

One of the most difficult things in animal photography is the constant movement of the subject which requires continuous focusing. While waiting for the critical moment to snap the shutter, I constantly focus the camera so that I can take the picture instantaneously.

Indoors the use of flash gives adequate illumination to the subject and also color temperature of the light corresponding to the daylight color film that should be used. Dependence on available light indoors would require such a low **f** stop with long exposure time that a tripod would be required. And, undoubtedly the color temperature of the light would be such that "off-colored" photographs would result.

In the outdoors, where the natural, available light is sufficient for correct exposure, I still almost always use a flash. While under these circumstances the flash does not contribute to the overall exposure, it does give a single high light in the eyes which I find desirable.

BIBLIOGRAPHY

Austin, Oliver L., Jr., **Birds of the World.** New York: Golden Press, 1983.

Catcott, E.J., D.V.M., Ph.D., editor. **Feline Medicine and Surgery.** Wheaton, IL: American Veterinary Publications, Inc. 1964.

Meyer, Alfred, **A Zoo for All Seasons.** Washington, D.C. Smithsonian Exposition Books, 1979.

Nilsson, Greta, **The Endangered Species Handbook.** Washington, D.C.: Animal Welfare Institute, 1983.

Reighard, Jacob and Jennings, H.S., 3rd Edition, Elliot, Rush, **Anatomy of the Cat.** New York: Henry Holt and Co., 1935.

Ripley, S. Dillon, **Zoo Book.** Washington, D.C.: Smithsonian Institution Press, 1976.

Tongren, Sally, **What's for Lunch.** New York: GMG Publishing 1981.

Walker, Ernest P., **Mammals of the World.** Baltimore: The Johns Hopkins Press, 1964.